American Diabetes Association

Forbidden
foods
Diabetic Cooking

DISCARDED

Maggie Powers, MS, RD, CDE
Joyce Hendley, MS

Director, Book Publishing, John Fedor; *Editor,* Laurie Guffey; *Production Manager,* Peggy M. Rote; *Composition,* Circle Graphics; *Cover Design,* KSA Group, Inc.; *Nutrient Analysis,* Nutritional Computing Consultants, Inc.; *Printer,* Transcontinental Printing, Inc.

Printed in Canada
3 5 7 9 10 8 6 4

The suggestions and information contained in this publication are generally consistent with the *Clinical Practice Recommendations* and other policies of the American Diabetes Association, but they do not represent the policy or position of the Association or any of its boards or committees. Reasonable steps have been taken to ensure the accuracy of the information presented. However, the American Diabetes Association cannot ensure the safety or efficacy of any product or service described in this publication. Individuals are advised to consult a physician or other appropriate health care professional before undertaking any diet or exercise program or taking any medication referred to in this publication. Professionals must use and apply their own professional judgment, experience, and training and should not rely solely on the information contained in this publication before prescribing any diet, exercise, or medication. The American Diabetes Association—its officers, directors, employees, volunteers, and members—assumes no responsibility or liability for personal or other injury, loss, or damage that may result from the suggestions or information in this publication.

♾ The paper in this publication meets the requirements of the ANSI Standard Z39.48-1992 (permanence of paper).

ADA titles may be purchased for business or promotional use or for special sales. To purchase this book in large quantities, or for custom editions of this book with your logo, contact Lee Romano Sequeira, Special Sales &Promotions, at the address below, or at LRomano@diabetes.org or 703-299-2046.

American Diabetes Association
1701 North Beauregard Street
Alexandria, VA 22311

Library of Congress Cataloging-in-Publication Data
Powers, Margaret.
    Forbidden Foods Diabetic Cooking / Maggie Powers and Joyce Hendley.
        p. cm.
    Includes index.
    ISBN 1-58040-045-0 (pbk. : alk. paper)
        1. Diabetes—Diet therapy—Recipes.   I. Hendley, Joyce, 1960.   II. Title.

RC662 .P69 2000
616.4'620654—dc21   00-061816

*T*his book belongs to all people living with diabetes, who know that eating is one of life's greatest pleasures. From you we have learned that no food needs to be forbidden!

Contents

Acknowledgments

WE WOULD LIKE TO THANK the American Diabetes Association for supporting the focus and publication of this cookbook, and each other for a wonderful collaboration and friendship!

Maggie thanks Colleen Geary Carter and her husband Bill and children Patrick, Mark, and Bridget for a number of special recipes contributed to this book; her family members Mike, Jessica, Colin, and Martin, who provided support, valuable comments, and the willingness to consume leftovers; her clients with diabetes who inspire her to create great-tasting food; and her local and national colleagues who spark her excitement for new ventures and enthusiastically encourage creativity.

Joyce thanks her guiding lights in the kitchen, whose work should be on everyone's shelves: Alice Medrich, author of *Chocolate and the Art of Low-Fat Baking*; Susan Purdy, author of *Have Your Cake and Eat It, Too*; Shirley Corriher, author of *Cookwise*; and especially Patsy Jamieson and the other talented cooks at the late, great *Eating Well* magazine. Joyce also thanks her family, Henrik, Maraika, and Peter, who put up with her crazy schedules and cheerfully accepted recipe outtakes; her friends and neighbors, whose willing stomachs and honest opinions made the recipes the best they could be; and the Think Tank group that sparked the collaboration that led to this book.

A Note about Food Labels

MANY FOOD LABELS IN THE GROCERY STORE use terms that can be confusing. To help you shop and eat better, here is a list of the common terms as defined by the Food and Drug Administration.

Sugar

Sugar Free: Less than 0.5 gram of sugar per serving.

No Added Sugar, Without Added Sugar, No Sugar Added: This does not mean the same as "sugar free." A label bearing these words means that no sugars were added during processing, or that processing does not increase the sugar content above the amount the ingredients naturally contain. Consult the nutrition information panel to see the total amount of sugar in this product.

Reduced Sugar: At least 25% less sugar per serving than the regular product.

Calories

Calorie Free: Fewer than 5 calories per serving.

Low Calorie: 40 calories or less per serving. (If servings are smaller than 30 grams, or smaller than 2 tablespoons, this means 40 calories or less per 50 grams of food.)

Reduced Calorie, Fewer Calories: At least 25% fewer calories per serving than the regular product.

Fat

Fat Free, Nonfat: Less than 0.5 gram of fat per serving.

Low Fat: 3 grams or less of fat per serving. (If servings are smaller than 30 grams, or smaller than 2 tablespoons, this means 3 grams or less of fat per 50 grams of food.)

Reduced Fat, Less Fat: At least 25% less fat per serving than the regular product.

Cholesterol

Cholesterol Free: Less than 2 milligrams of cholesterol, and 2 grams or less of saturated fat per serving.
Low Cholesterol: 20 milligrams or less of cholesterol, and 2 grams or less of saturated fat per serving.
Reduced Cholesterol, Less Cholesterol: At least 25% less cholesterol, and 2 grams or less of saturated fat per serving than the regular product.

Sodium

Sodium Free: Less than 5 milligrams of sodium per serving.
Low Sodium: 140 milligrams or less of sodium per serving.
Very Low Sodium: 35 milligrams or less of sodium per serving.
Reduced Sodium, Less Sodium: At least 25% less sodium per serving than the regular product.

Light or Lite Foods

Foods that are labeled "Light" or "Lite" are usually either lower in fat or lower in calories than the regular product. Some products may also be lower in sodium. Check the nutrition information label on the back of the product to make sure.

Meat and Poultry

Lean: Less than 10 grams of fat, 4.5 grams or less of saturated fat, and less than 95 milligrams of cholesterol per serving and per 100 grams.
Extra Lean: Less than 5 grams of fat, less than 2 grams of saturated fat, and less than 95 milligrams of cholesterol per serving and per 100 grams.

ntroduction

MANY FOODS ARE PART OF OUR PERSONAL HISTORY and have followed us on our journey through life. Our life experiences include living in a certain area, having family of a particular background, living with others who influence our choices, and adapting to new lifestyles and schedules. Because of these experiences, we like to have certain foods at holidays, birthdays, and other celebrations. Special foods are part of our traditions, traditions we want to maintain and pass on to others. Many of us have favorite recipes we want to share with our family and friends. Just because you have diabetes, you don't want to give up this part of who you are—and you don't have to!

This cookbook will help you learn how to cook and enjoy your favorite foods, even though you have diabetes. You may think these foods are forbidden and that you need to cheat in order to eat them. Not true! If you have diabetes, you can still have scrumptious desserts and special main-dish favorites, as long as you account for any extra carbohydrate and fat in your total daily meal plan.

New Recipe Solutions

We have developed 150 great-tasting recipes for you, but what if we missed one or more of your favorites? We can teach you how to modify your own family recipes to make them healthier without losing the flavor you love. Our Recipe Solution Tips focus on four magic ingredients—fat, sugar, salt, and flavorings. We can show you ways to replace or reduce fat, sugar, and salt, and increase or change flavorings to give your personal recipes an easy makeover!

A Little Background

Each ingredient in a recipe is carefully chosen for the job it does and the taste it gives. The table below summarizes what ingredients do in a recipe. Sometimes an easy switch can be made, but not always. When making replacements, you're looking for ingredients that can do the same job but in a healthier way. Also, when you change the amount of one ingredient you may need to change the amount of another ingredient.

Fat Provides	Sugar Provides	Salt Provides	Flavoring Provides
Flavor	Sweetness	Saltiness	Flavor
Enhanced taste	Structure, bulk, volume	Enhanced taste	
Rich and creamy texture	Texture	Longer shelf life	
Smell	Color, browning, caramelization		
Heat stability	Moistness and tenderness		
Moistness	Lowers freezing point		
Tenderness	Longer shelf life		
Body, height, fluffiness			
Even blending of other ingredients (emulsification)			

Know Your Ingredients

It is important to know the source of fat, sugar, salt, and flavorings in recipes if you plan to do a recipe makeover. The following list will help you be an informed cook.

Sources of Fat	Sources of Sugar	Sources of Salt	Sources of Flavoring
Avocados	Brown sugar	Table salt	Spices
Bacon	Corn syrup	Baking soda	Herbs
Butter	Fruit juice	Bouillon, broth, consommé	Extracts
Coconut	Granulated (white) sugar	Pickles	
Cream	Powdered sugar	Seasoning salts	
Drippings	Molasses	Soy sauce	
Lard		Olives	
Margarine		Canned foods	
Mayonnaise		Processed meats	
Oils: safflower, soybean, sunflower, canola, corn, olive		Cheese	
Peanut butter			
Nuts			
Seeds			
Shortening			
Processed meats			
Whole milk products: cheese, sour cream, ice cream			

Here's the Math

You can often reduce the amount of an ingredient and replace it with something healthier without compromising taste, but how do you know how much to leave out? The table on the next page is a handy reference to use when you're reducing ingredient amounts. We will give you suggestions about reducing the amount of fat, sugar, or salt by 1/4, 1/3, or 1/2. Use the table to see how much of that ingredient to use instead.

Usual Amount	1/4 Less	1/3 Less	1/2 Less
1 cup	3/4 cup	2/3 cup	1/2 cup
3/4 cup	1/2 cup + 1 Tbsp	1/2 cup	1/3 cup + 2 tsp
2/3 cup	1/2 cup	1/3 cup + 2 Tbsp	1/3 cup
1/2 cup	1/4 cup + 2 Tbsp	1/3 cup	1/4 cup
1/3 cup	1/4 cup	3 Tbsp + 2 tsp	2 Tbsp + 2 tsp
1/4 cup	3 Tbsp	2 Tbsp + 2 tsp	2 Tbsp (1/8 cup)
1 Tbsp	2 1/4 tsp	2 tsp	1 1/2 tsp

Tips to Reduce Fat

A Brief Word about Fat

All natural fats have the same number of calories—9 calories per gram, 100 calories per tablespoon, and 1,600 calories per cup. Margarine has the same amount of calories as butter, teaspoon for teaspoon, cup for cup. Oils have essentially the same number of calories as margarine and butter. Even a teaspoon of meat fat has the same number of calories as other fats.

Now, if you take some fat and whip it you can decrease the calories . . . a little. Using whipped fat in cooking takes some care. The fat melts, the air leaves, and you have less fat—and less volume. The same goes for diet spreads and margarines, because they contain more water than their full-fat counterparts. Heat them and the water evaporates, again leaving you with less volume and soggy baked goods. That's why you can't substitute whipped or diet fats and expect the recipe to work the same way.

Yes, You Do Need Fat

First, let's be clear—all people need fat in their diets. Fat can not only add great flavor to foods, it really is a necessary part of a healthy eating plan, as it provides key nutrients and helps you feel satisfied with a meal. However, it's the *type* and *amount* of fat you eat that you need to watch.

Our recipes call for a variety of fats. Different fats are used because of their different tastes and cooking properties, such as the flavor and texture they provide. Can you think of how chocolate chip cookies would differ in look and taste when made with canola oil, olive oil, shortening, bacon fat, liquid butter, regular butter, or margarine? We tend to use the fats that are lower in cholesterol, yet have included small amounts of other fats to keep the flavors great. Sometimes a small amount of flavor-rich butter does more than less tasty margarine.

Ways to Reduce Fat

The challenge in recipe development is to reduce fat just enough so you don't compromise taste, looks, and tenderness. Our belief is that healthy food should taste great. We've done the experimenting with our recipes to find the right blend of ingredients and best cooking methods. You can do this with your recipes, too!

Omit, Reduce, or Replace

It is easy to omit fat in some recipes, but not so easy in others. Sometimes just a little fat makes the magic work.

In fried foods

■ **Omit** fat by using a different cooking method. You can bake, grill, or broil without fat. Broiling and grilling are great because the fat drips away from the food while it cooks. Try oven roasting — simply toss meatballs, burgers, cubed stew meat, or cut-up vegetables with a little oil and brown on a rack in a roasting pan in a hot (400°F) oven. Or make crispy-coated chicken or fish — dip each piece in egg white, then cornflakes or bread crumbs, and bake in a 400°F oven — for great flavor without the fat.

- **Reduce** fat by using less to get the same effect without the greasy result. Sauté with 1–2 tsp of oil in a nonstick pan rather than 1–2 Tbsp and you can save over 200 calories.

- **Replace** fat with a nonstick cooking spray or parchment paper. Spray cooking pans with nonstick cooking spray or line a cooking sheet with parchment paper to prevent sticking.

In casseroles

- It is difficult to **omit** the fat entirely in these foods, but you can try using fat-free broth, fat-free yogurt, fat-free mayonnaise, or fat-free sour cream. (Yogurt and sour cream can separate when heated, so add them to hot dishes at the end of the cooking time.)

- **Reduce** fat by using a low-fat alternative such as low-fat soups, low-fat mayonnaise, and low-fat sour cream. Also, choose low-fat meat cuts, take the skin off of poultry, and use low-fat cheeses. (Since low-fat cheeses often don't melt well, add them at the end of cooking if you can, and cook just enough to heat through. Most work best when grated and sprinkled on the top of a dish.)

In baked desserts

Baked foods such as breads, cookies, and cakes use fat to add lightness to the food, so adjusting the fat content in these types of recipes is a bit trickier.

- **Omit** fat if the batter can be lightened with something else. For example, in our granola bars, we replaced the butter in the original recipe with orange juice to provide moistness and a flavor boost.

- **Reduce** fat by 1/4 or 1/3 as a starting point; you can probably get away without having to change anything further. However, if you find the batter is too heavy, you can compensate by using a little less flour, or by replacing some or all of the flour with cake flour. Also, it's especially important not to overmix batter that is lower in fat—it just makes it heavier.

- **Replace** some of the fat with a fruit purée, such as applesauce, prune butter, or jarred baby food fruits. We use applesauce in our chocolate brownie recipe, and puréed apricots in our apricot bars. You can replace a cup of oil, butter, margarine, or shortening with a cup of applesauce; or in cake, muffin, or quick bread recipes, replace butter or oil with a combination of half applesauce and half buttermilk.

More Ways to Reduce Fat

- Try leaving the fat out of sandwiches—you'll miss it less because of the other tasty ingredients. Order a fast food sandwich with no sauce or make a sandwich with spicy mustard and extra vegetables—you won't miss the mayonnaise.

- Forget the butter or margarine on noodles, rice, potatoes, and green beans. Enjoy the real taste of these foods or sprinkle on some great spices. If you'd like a light sauce, try broth, tomato sauce, low-fat sour cream, or fat-free ranch dressing.

- Make it a habit to use low-fat choices when making dressings and sauces. You can easily substitute low-fat or fat-free milk, sour cream, cheese, and soup in recipes. We use low-fat (1%) milk in our recipes. If you like, you can reduce the fat a bit more by using fat-free (skim) milk. The recipes still taste great with this slight reduction in fat.

■ Bring out the flavor of other ingredients. Cooking onions, garlic, and other vegetables in a nonstick pan or in a small amount of fat before adding them in heightens their taste dramatically in the final food. Many spices, such as cumin, coriander, and chili powder, taste better if you toast them first in a dry skillet. Nuts, too, are more flavorful when heated; by toasting them first, you can use fewer of them in a recipe.

■ Add heavy ingredients late in the cooking process. Since both fat and sugar keep batters light and help them rise in the oven, a reduced-fat, reduced-sugar recipe needs extra help. For example, the chopped apricots are added halfway through the cooking process in our apricot bars, as are the chocolate chips in our chocolate cherry bars, so that the batter has a chance to rise on its own first.

Tips to Reduce Sugar
Yes, You Can Eat Some Sugar!

Have you heard? It's the total carbohydrate that usually matters most in your meal plan, not the source of carbohydrate. Sugar, fruits, vegetables, and grains are all sources of carbohydrate. Of course, fruits, vegetables, and grains have lots more nutrients and fiber than sugar does, calorie for calorie. But the days when you, as a person with diabetes, had to completely avoid sugar are over. Now you need to know how to balance the sugar you want to eat with the other carbohydrates in your daily meal plan. That means you can sit down with a dietitian and figure out how to have some of your favorite foods and still follow a healthy meal plan!

A little bit of sugar is needed in breads to help yeast grow, in tomato products to cut the acidity, and in some preserved meats to add moisture and extend shelf life. In baked products, sugar gives a great sweet taste and adds tenderness and, often, a brown crispy crust. Taking out too much sugar can result in a heavy, bland product. However, many traditional versions of recipes are so high in sugar that you can take out a lot without altering the flavor very much—and many people prefer the newer flavor.

What about Low-Calorie Sweeteners?

The four low-calorie sweeteners currently approved for use in the U.S. are acesulfame-K, aspartame, saccharin, and sucralose. They are all considered low-calorie sweeteners because they give a food or beverage a sweet taste with few or no added calories. Many people with diabetes use the tabletop versions of these sweeteners in place of the old-fashioned sugar bowl with granulated sugar.

You can use low-calorie sweeteners in recipes, but some hold up better than others when heated, so check the package instructions. You can also blend the sweeteners—using half of one and half of another, for example—to balance desired taste and performance. Sometimes you can make an easy substitution, but other times you need to change other ingredients to maintain the bulk, texture, browning, and softness of a food. Try some experiments in your own kitchen!

Ways to Reduce Sugar

When sugar is greatly reduced, it is difficult to get the food to develop the brown color that we expect. For some of those foods, cooking at a high temperature for a brief amount of time can compensate for the decrease in sugar.

Omit, Reduce, or Replace

In sauces and spreads

■ **Omit** sugar if the recipe tastes just as great without it. For example, many of our appetizers do not have any sugar added. Your favorite recipe might not need it either—try it and see!

■ **Reduce** sugar if only a little is needed. For example, many tomato sauces have just a small amount of granulated sugar added to decrease the acidity. If your recipe calls for more than 1–2 tsp per 2 cups of sauce, try decreasing to that amount. If the sugar is in a sweet sauce, try using ripe fruit or a reduced-sugar substitute. We use a reduced-sugar pie filling in our chocolate cherry bars, and our apple crisp calls for fresh fruit so you can enjoy the natural taste of the apples rather than overwhelming sweetness.

■ **Replace** sugar with other flavorings or a stronger version of the existing flavorings. For example, in many of our chocolate recipes we use several forms of chocolate—cocoa, chocolate chips, baking chocolate, and sometimes coffee, which has a chocolate-like bitterness. These build layers of chocolate flavor, creating richness without a lot of calories or fat.

In baked goods

■ **Omit** sugar if the recipe has enough fruit to stand on its own. A pie or cobbler made with very ripe fruit might not need any sugar in the filling.

■ **Reduce** sugar easily by 1/4, probably by 1/3, or perhaps by 1/2. You'll have to experiment. If you take out too much sugar, desserts may not rise, be less tender, or be bland in looks and flavor. Switching to less of a superfine sugar helps keep the dessert light.

■ **Replace** some sugar with other flavorings or a stronger version of current flavorings. For example, adding a small amount of cinnamon perks up chocolate chip cookies without a detectable cinnamon taste, and using double-strength vanilla extract (available from specialty spice companies) adds extra-delicious flavor to any cookies. In fact, using spices we normally associate with sweet foods, like vanilla, nutmeg, cloves, or cinnamon, can boost the illusion of sweetness without adding any sugar.

Other Ways to Reduce Sugar

- Sprinkle the sugar on top or in a glaze, as we did in our cinnamon rolls and the orange chiffon cake. Since it's the first thing you taste, you really get a wallop in every bite from just a little sugar on top.

- Use honey instead of sugar in non-baked items, like sweet drinks. Its flavor is more intense so you only need a little, even though spoonful for spoonful it has the same amount of carbohydrate and calories as other sugars.

Tips to Reduce Salt

Salt does more than give a salty taste—it enhances other flavors. Often just a little bit of salt in a recipe goes a long way. You may find, though, that in some recipes you don't need any salt. For example, we don't recommend adding salt to water when cooking pasta or rice.

If you are used to eating foods high in salt, it may take some time before you retrain your taste buds to appreciate less salt. After a while, foods with less salt really will taste better to you. If you find some of the recipes in this cookbook too low in salt, you can always add a bit more to your own serving, if your meal plan permits it. Studies show you'll probably end up using less salt in the long run if you only add it at the table: sprinkled on top, salt has more of a taste impact than when it is cooked into a food. You may also want to examine your other food choices and try to decrease your overall salt intake so you can enjoy occasional salty foods.

When you decrease salt in a recipe, you may need to boost other flavorings or adjust the cooking method to bring out more of the flavors already there. One of the best ways to create the illusion of salt is to add an acidic ingredient, such as lemon juice or vinegar. These seem to bring out the food's own salty flavors. Try sprinkling lemon juice on your green beans or vinegar on your French fries, and you may find additional salt unnecessary.

Tips to Increase Flavor

Do you know how long your spices have been in your spice cabinet? Do some of your spice containers look like antiques? It is amazing how nonchalant we are with such critical ingredients as spices. Most spices lose their flavor within a year. You'll be amazed at the difference fresh spices make in your cooking.

You'll also find that when recipes are lower in fat, sugar, and salt, like ours, the natural flavors of the ingredients shine through. You may need to add fewer flavorings than the recipe originally called for, or more after you reduce unwanted fat or sugar. For best results, try some of the hints below.

- Use fresh herbs, specialty spices, and pure flavoring extracts when available, as their flavors are more intense.

- Increase the amount of spices already in the recipe.

- Add seasonings at the right time in the cooking process. Often basil and other fresh herbs do better when added towards the end of the cooking time, so their flavor remains strong. Also add dried, delicate herbs like chervil or marjoram later. Some examples of spices that should be added earlier, so their flavors will develop more, are cumin, coriander, allspice, nutmeg, and ginger.

■ Select seasonings that will enhance flavors that are already in the recipe. Examples include nutmeg, which goes well with the buttery flavor of creamy dishes, and fresh chopped parsley, which is delicious in tomato-based dishes and soups and brings out the flavors of other dried herbs.

A Word about Carbohydrates and Nutritional Analysis

When you look at the exchange values for the following recipes, sometimes you will see the word "starch" and sometimes the word "carbohydrate." Foods from the Exchange Lists Carbohydrate Group (starch, fruit, milk, and other carbohydrates) may be interchanged, as each group contains about 15 grams of carbohydrate. Most desserts, sweet snacks, and low-fat dressings, are carbohydrate exchanges. Other foods with carbohydrate are categorized as starch, fruit, milk, or vegetable exchanges. For more explanation of exchange groups, see *Exchange Lists for Meal Planning*, available from the American Diabetes Association.

Better Beverages

Recipes

Holiday Nog

Preparation time: 5 minutes
Cooking time: none
Serves: 4   Serving size: 3/4 cup

Not so long ago eggnog was made by blending raw eggs and cream together to make a very rich, thick beverage. Rum and nutmeg were often added to the adult drink. Today, food safety experts discourage drinking or consuming raw eggs at any time. (Purchased eggnog contains pasteurized eggs to eliminate any safety concerns.) Here, though, we've used soy drink and bananas, making a delightful taste while dramatically boosting the nutrition. Try it!

> 1 cup plain soy drink
> 1 cup orange juice
> 1 medium banana
> 1 tsp vanilla extract
> 8 ice cubes
> 1/2 tsp ground allspice

In a blender, combine the soy drink, juice, banana, vanilla, and ice cubes until smooth. Pour into glasses and sprinkle with the allspice.

Soy drink is a lactose-free, milk-like product that has been fortified with calcium and other nutrients to make it fairly comparable nutritionally to cow's milk. It smells and looks slightly different than cow's milk, so don't be surprised when you first open it! After opening, you need to use it within 7–10 days—try making more Holiday Nog, a Strawberry Smoothie (see recipe, page 25), or pouring it on your breakfast cereal.

Exchanges
1 Carbohydrate

Calories 78
   Calories from Fat . . . 5
Total Fat . . . . 1 g
   Saturated Fat . . . . . . 0 g
Cholesterol . . . . 0 mg
Sodium . . . . 23 mg
Carbohydrate . . . . . . 17 g
   Dietary Fiber . . . . . . 1 g
   Sugars . . . . 13 g
Protein . . . . 2 g

Hot Chocolate

Preparation time: 3 minutes
Cooking time: none
Serves: 1   Serving size: 1 cup

Brrrrrrr! Some days just call for hot chocolate. Although this recipe makes one serving, you can easily double or triple it when friends come by. Use the best quality unsweetened cocoa powder that you can find. For extra flavor, crush a small peppermint hard candy in the hot cocoa and stir to blend.

> 1 cup fat-free milk, heated
> 2 Tbsp confectioners sugar
> 2 tsp unsweetened cocoa powder
> 1/8 tsp vanilla extract

In a small saucepan, heat the milk over medium heat, stirring occasionally, until bubbles appear at the sides of the pan, 2 minutes. Whisk in the sugar, cocoa, and vanilla until smooth.

Exchanges
1 Carbohydrate
1 Fat-Free Milk

Calories 154
  Calories from Fat . . . 8
Total Fat . . . . 1 g
  Saturated Fat . . . . . . 0 g
Cholesterol . . . . 4 mg
Sodium . . . . 126 mg
Carbohydrate . . . . . . 29 g
  Dietary Fiber . . . . . . 1 g
  Sugars . . . . 26 g
Protein . . . . 9 g

Iced Cappuccino Smoothie

Preparation time: 5 minutes
Cooking time: none
Serves: 8   Serving size: 1 1/2 cups

Love the creamy coffee shakes at Café Yuppée but not the calories (or the price tag)? You'll love this homemade version. Prepare the mix in minutes (the recipe easily doubles) and store it in an airtight container in the pantry. Just whirl a little mix with ice and milk in the blender when the smoothie mood strikes.

Smoothie Mix
- 1/2 cup fat-free vanilla-flavored coffee creamer
- 1/3 cup instant coffee crystals
- 1/3 cup instant fat-free milk powder
- 1/4 cup granulated sugar

Combine all ingredients in a blender and pulse several times until finely powdered and well blended. Store in an airtight container up to 3 months.

Single Smoothie
- 1/2 cup fat-free (skim) milk
- 2 Tbsp Smoothie Mix
- 6–8 ice cubes

Combine the milk and Smoothie Mix in a blender; whirl until smooth. Add ice cubes and pulse until thick and creamy.

Exchanges

(for Smoothie Mix)
1 Carbohydrate

Serving Size	2 Tbsp
Calories	55
Calories from Fat	0
Total Fat	0 g
Saturated Fat	0 g
Cholesterol	0 mg
Sodium	20 mg
Carbohydrate	12 g
Dietary Fiber	0 g
Sugars	9 g
Protein	1 g

Exchanges

(for Single Smoothie)
1 Carbohydrate

Calories	98
Calories from Fat	2
Total Fat	0 g
Saturated Fat	0 g
Cholesterol	3 mg
Sodium	83 mg
Carbohydrate	18 g
Dietary Fiber	0 g
Sugars	14 g
Protein	5 g

Party Punch

Preparation time: 5 minutes
Cooking time: none
Serves: 4–6   Serving size: 3/4 cup

You'll love the combination of juices used here! The cranberry-apple juice gives this punch pretty color, while the pineapple packs the flavor punch. To make a frosty drink, fill some special glasses and pop them in the freezer for 30–60 minutes before serving.

  2   cups low-calorie cranberry-apple juice, chilled
1 1/2   cups diet lemon-lime soda, chilled
  1   cup unsweetened pineapple juice, chilled
  1   orange, thinly sliced
      Ice cubes

In a large punch bowl, combine the cranberry juice, soda, and pineapple juice. Add the ice cubes, then top with the orange slices.

All fruit should be washed well before using, especially if you add it to a food like this punch.

Exchanges
1 Fruit

Calories 57
  Calories from Fat . . . 1
Total Fat . . . . 0 g
  Saturated Fat . . . . . . 0 g
Cholesterol . . . . 0 mg
Sodium . . . . 35 mg
Carbohydrate . . . . . . 14 g
  Dietary Fiber . . . . . . 1 g
  Sugars . . . . 13 g
Protein . . . . 0 g

Peppermint Punch

Preparation time: 5 minutes
Cooking time: none
Serves: 1   Serving size: 3/4 cup

Kids and adults will love the taste of this delightful red, minty punch. Serve it immediately, or make it and put it in the freezer for an hour for a frozen treat.

3/4 cup grapefruit diet soda
1 drop red food coloring
1 Tbsp vanilla frozen yogurt
1/2 round peppermint candy, crushed

Pour the soda into a small glass and stir in the food coloring. Top with the yogurt and sprinkle with candy to serve.

We used peppermint candy that was individually packaged, crushed it with a hammer, then sprinkled half on the yogurt. You can easily double or triple this recipe for additional servings or make a big batch in a punch bowl.

Exchanges
Free Food

Calories 17
  Calories from Fat . . . 3
Total Fat . . . . 0 g
  Saturated Fat . . . . . . 0 g
Cholesterol . . . . 1 mg
Sodium . . . . 14 mg
Carbohydrate . . . . 3 g
  Dietary Fiber . . . . . . 0 g
  Sugars . . . . 3 g
Protein . . . . 1 g

Piña Colada

Preparation time: 2 minutes
Cooking time: none
Serves: 4   Serving size: 1/2 cup

Piña Coladas are reminders of hot, lazy days, but you can enjoy this nonalcoholic, nutritious version any time of the year! If you miss the rum taste, add 1/2 tsp of rum extract when you are blending.

         1 8-oz carton Piña Colada-flavored yogurt
       1/2 cup unsweetened pineapple juice
       1/2 cup low-fat (1%) milk
         5 ice cubes

In a blender, add the yogurt, juice, milk, and ice cubes and blend until smooth, 1–2 minutes.

Exchanges
1 Carbohydrate

Calories 88
    Calories from Fat . . . 8
Total Fat . . . . 1 g
    Saturated Fat . . . . . . 1 g
Cholesterol . . . . 6 mg
Sodium . . . . 47 mg
Carbohydrate . . . . . . 17 g
    Dietary Fiber . . . . . . 0 g
    Sugars . . . . 15 g
Protein . . . . 3 g

Lemon Tea Cooler

Preparation time: 2 minutes
Cooking time: none
Serves: 4   Serving size: 3/4 cup

So simple, yet so refreshing! The pineapple juice and tea make a great duo in this cooler. Use bottled tea or make your own. Two servings equals a fruit serving, which brings you one step closer to your five-a-day.

2 cups diet lemon-flavored tea, chilled
1 cup unsweetened pineapple juice, chilled
8 ice cubes

In a pitcher, combine the tea, juice, and ice cubes. Garnish with a thin lemon wedge or a small sprig of mint leaves.

Exchanges
1/2 Fruit

Calories 36
　Calories from Fat . . . 0
Total Fat . . . . 0 g
　Saturated Fat . . . . . . 0 g
Cholesterol . . . . 0 mg
Sodium . . . . 4 mg
Carbohydrate . . . . . . 9 g
　Dietary Fiber . . . . . . 0 g
　Sugars . . . . 8 g
Protein . . . . 0 g

Tomato Sparkler

Preparation time: 5 minutes
Cooking time: none
Serves: 1   Serving size: 3/4 cup

There are many ways to make a Bloody Mary; in fact, whole books are devoted to versions of the basic tomato and rum beverage. Our modest version, with the ever-present celery stalk, packs quite a punch. You can add more hot sauce for your own special tang, if you like.

1/2 cup reduced-sodium vegetable juice, chilled
1/4 cup club soda, chilled
     Dash hot sauce
     Minced cilantro to taste
1/2 stalk celery

In a small glass, combine the juice and soda. Stir in the hot sauce, then sprinkle with the cilantro. Place the celery in the glass and serve.

Exchanges
1 Vegetable

Calories 26
   Calories from Fat . . . 1
Total Fat . . . . 0 g
   Saturated Fat . . . . . . 0 g
Cholesterol . . . . 0 mg
Sodium . . . . 60 mg
Carbohydrate . . . . . . 6 g
   Dietary Fiber . . . . . . 1 g
   Sugars . . . . 4 g
Protein . . . . 1 g

Strawberry Smoothie

Preparation time: 3 minutes
Cooking time: none
Serves: 6 Serving size: 1/2 cup

A fruit smoothie can be a tasty breakfast or after-school snack, and it's packed with nutrition! If you think they are way too complicated to make, give this one a try. The unsweetened frozen fruit found in your grocery store makes this a year-round treat. Don't thaw the fruit; just toss it in the blender with the other ingredients.

1 cup fat-free vanilla-flavored yogurt
1 cup frozen unsweetened strawberries
1/2 cup low-fat (1%) milk
1/4 cup orange juice
2 Tbsp wheat germ
1 tsp vanilla extract
10 ice cubes

In a blender or food processor, puree all the ingredients until smooth, about 1–1 1/2 minutes.

You can easily substitute other frozen fruit such as raspberries, blueberries, or mixed fruit for this smoothie.

Exchanges
1/2 Carbohydrate

Calories 55
 Calories from Fat . . . 4
Total Fat . . . . 0 g
 Saturated Fat . . . . . . 0 g
Cholesterol . . . . 2 mg
Sodium . . . . 39 mg
Carbohydrate . . . . . . 10 g
 Dietary Fiber . . . . . . 1 g
 Sugars . . . . 7 g
Protein . . . . 3 g

Starters & Snacks

Recipes

Caramel Crunch Popcorn

Preparation time: 5 minutes
Cooking time: 10 minutes
Serves: 24   Serving size: 1/2 cup

In this recipe, a little caramel flavor goes a long way. Although the serving size is small, there's plenty of satisfying sweet taste and crunchy texture. This recipe makes a big batch and can be stored in an airtight container and kept for about 1 week.

> 12 cups plain air-popped popcorn (about 1 cup unpopped)
> 1 cup granulated sugar
> 10 Tbsp stick margarine
> 1/3 cup light corn syrup
> 1 tsp vanilla extract

1. Cover 2 baking sheets with aluminum foil and spray with nonstick cooking spray. Spread the popped popcorn on the baking sheets in a single layer.

2. In a medium nonstick skillet, combine the sugar, margarine, and syrup. Bring to a boil over medium heat, stirring constantly, about 3 minutes. Continue cooking and stirring until the mixture turns a light caramel color, 5 minutes; do not overcook or the caramel will brown and burn! Remove from the heat and slowly stir in the vanilla.

3. Pour the caramel mixture over the popcorn. When the caramel has cooled, break it into bite-size pieces.

Exchanges

1 Carbohydrate
1 Fat

Calories	109
Calories from Fat	44
Total Fat	5 g
Saturated Fat	1 g
Cholesterol	0 mg
Sodium	63 mg
Carbohydrate	17 g
Dietary Fiber	1 g
Sugars	12 g
Protein	0 g

Chiles Rellenos

Preparation time: 20 minutes
Cooking time: 30 minutes
Serves: 6   Serving size: 1 chile relleno

These stuffed chile peppers are traditionally dipped in batter and fried, but they're just as tasty roasted. For a more substantial meal, wrap a chile relleno in a warmed flour tortilla and eat it like a sandwich.

    6 poblano chili peppers
    1 tsp canola oil
    2 green onions, white and green parts, minced
    1 clove garlic, minced
    1 cup low-fat ricotta cheese
    1 cup shredded low-fat mozzarella cheese
       Chopped cilantro, for garnish

To prepare the chiles:

1. Place the broiler pan 4–6 inches from the heat source and preheat the broiler.

2. Line a baking sheet with foil and place the chiles on the baking sheet. Broil, turning frequently with tongs, until the skin is lightly charred on all sides, about 10 minutes. Remove from the oven, transfer to a paper bag, fold the bag closed, and let stand 10 minutes.

3. Peel the cooked chiles over the sink to drain the juices. Make a slit in the side of each chile and carefully remove the seeds and veins, keeping the stem intact. Pat dry. (The chiles may be prepared ahead of time, wrapped in plastic, and refrigerated up to 2 days.)

To assemble the chiles rellenos:

1. Preheat the oven to 325°F. Line a baking sheet with foil and spray with nonstick cooking spray.

2. In a small skillet, heat the oil. Cook the onions and garlic, stirring as needed, until the onions are softened, 3 minutes.

Exchanges

1 Lean Meat
2 Vegetable
1 Fat

Calories 146
  Calories from Fat . . 65
Total Fat . . . . 7 g
  Saturated Fat . . . . . . 4 g
Cholesterol . . . . 23 mg
Sodium . . . . 146 mg
Carbohydrate . . . . . . 11 g
  Dietary Fiber . . . . . . 1 g
  Sugars . . . . 5 g
Protein . . . . 11 g

3. In a medium bowl, combine the ricotta and mozzarella cheeses with the onion mixture; set aside.

4. Stuff each chile with about 3 Tbsp of the cheese mixture. Press the sides together so the chiles appear closed and place them on a baking sheet. Bake until heated through, about 20 minutes. Sprinkle with the cilantro and serve immediately.

Poblano chili peppers, sometimes called pasillas, look like darker green versions of bell peppers, but with a wide stem end and a pointy tip. They can be found in most supermarkets and Latino grocery stores.

Deviled Eggs

Preparation time: 15 minutes
Cooking time: 15 minutes
Serves: 12   Serving: 2 egg halves

This old-fashioned picnic dish lost a lot of its fat and calories with the help of fat-free cottage cheese—a perfect stand-in for both the fatty egg yolk and the mayonnaise.

1	dozen large eggs
1/2	cup fat-free cottage cheese
3	Tbsp lite mayonnaise
2	Tbsp sweet pickle relish
1/2	tsp dry mustard
	Paprika, for garnish

1. Place the eggs in a large saucepan with enough cold water to cover by 1 inch. Bring to a simmer (do not boil!) and cook 10 minutes (start the timer as soon as the water bubbles). Drain and set the pan under cold running water for 2 minutes. Peel the eggs and slice them in half lengthwise. With a small spoon, carefully remove the yolks, reserving 6 yolks for another use.

2. In a blender, puree the cottage cheese until smooth; set aside.

3. In a medium bowl, mix the remaining 6 egg yolks with the cottage cheese mixture, mayonnaise, relish, and mustard; spoon the mixture back into the hollowed-out egg whites. Arrange the eggs on a platter and sprinkle with paprika.

Exchanges
1 Medium-Fat Meat

Calories 69
  Calories from Fat . . 34
Total Fat . . . . 4 g
  Saturated Fat . . . . . . 1 g
Cholesterol . . . . 108 mg
Sodium . . . . 143 mg
Carbohydrate . . . . 2 g
  Dietary Fiber . . . . . . 0 g
  Sugars . . . . 2 g
Protein . . . . 6 g

Garlic Bread

Preparation time: 20 minutes
Cooking time: 20 minutes
Serves: 12   Serving size: 2 slices

Here's proof that simpler is better. For a delightful variation that goes well with roasted pork or turkey, substitute crumbled dried sage leaves for the oregano.

- 4 Tbsp extra-virgin olive oil
- 2 Tbsp unsalted margarine or butter, melted
- 2 cloves garlic, minced
- 1/2 tsp dried oregano
- 1/4 tsp seasoned salt
- 1 1-lb loaf Italian or French bread, cut into 24 1/2-inch slices

1. Preheat the oven to 400°F.

2. In a small bowl, combine the oil, butter, garlic, oregano, and salt. Brush the mixture on one side of each bread slice, then press the slices back together to form a loaf. Wrap the loaf in foil and bake until hot in the center, 15–20 minutes.

Exchanges
1 1/2 Starch
1 Fat

Calories 148
    Calories from Fat . . 58
Total Fat . . . . 6 g
    Saturated Fat . . . . . . 1 g
Cholesterol . . . . 0 mg
Sodium . . . . 258 mg
Carbohydrate . . . . . . 19 g
    Dietary Fiber . . . . . . 1 g
    Sugars . . . . 0 g
Protein . . . . 4 g

Garlic Sticks

Preparation time: 10 minutes
Cooking time: 13 minutes
Serves: 4   Serving size: 5 sticks

These garlic sticks are an alternative to the high fat and salt versions. The best part is it's a way to use that day-old bread!

- 2 Tbsp extra-virgin olive oil
- 4 slices day-old white bread
- 2 Tbsp grated Parmesan cheese
- 2 cloves garlic, minced
- 1 tsp dried oregano

1. Preheat the oven to 375°F. Spray a baking sheet with nonstick cooking spray. Pour the oil into a small bowl.

2. Cut each slice of bread into 5 even strips, about 3/4 inch wide. Arrange on a piece of wax paper. Brush each strip lightly with the oil on both sides.

3. In a small bowl, combine the cheese, garlic, and oregano. Sprinkle this mixture over the strips, pressing with your fingers to make the crumb mixture adhere.

4. Place on the prepared baking sheet and bake until lightly browned, about 13 minutes.

Exchanges
1 Starch
1 1/2 Fat

Calories 144
  Calories from Fat . . 79
Total Fat . . . . 9 g
  Saturated Fat . . . . . . 0 g
Cholesterol . . . . 4 mg
Sodium . . . . 199 mg
Carbohydrate . . . . . . 13 g
  Dietary Fiber . . . . . . 1 g
  Sugars . . . . 2 g
Protein . . . . 4 g

Day-old bread isn't necessarily just a day old—it's a term that began when bread was homemade without preservatives and grew stale after a day or two. Feel free to use any bread that's been around long enough to have a firm texture—for some, that might be over a week. Rye, pumpernickel, and whole-wheat breads are delicious variations.

Guacamole

Preparation time: 20 minutes
Cooking time: none
Serves: 16 Serving size: 2 Tbsp

Yes, avocados are loaded with fat, but it's mostly the heart-healthy monounsaturated kind. More good news: you can enjoy them guilt-free in this cool, classic dip. Add more jalapeños if you're the heat-loving type. This guacamole is full of chunks and color, like the traditional version.

1	ripe medium avocado, peeled, pitted, and cut into chunks
1/4	cup fat-free sour cream
2	small plum tomatoes, diced
1/4	cup diced seedless cucumber
1/4	medium red onion, finely chopped
2	Tbsp chopped cilantro
2	Tbsp freshly squeezed lime juice
1–2	small jalapeño peppers, seeded and finely chopped
1/4	tsp seasoned salt

1. In a medium bowl with a fork, mash the avocado with the sour cream (there should be small chunks remaining).

2. Add the tomatoes, cucumber, onion, cilantro, lime juice, jalapeños, and salt; stir lightly until well blended.

Exchanges
1/2 Fat

Calories 28
  Calories from Fat . . 18
Total Fat . . . . 2 g
  Saturated Fat . . . . . . 1 g
Cholesterol . . . . 0 mg
Sodium . . . . 31 mg
Carbohydrate . . . . 3 g
  Dietary Fiber . . . . . . 1 g
  Sugars . . . . 1 g
Protein . . . . 1 g

This dip is best when served immediately. To store, cover the bowl with plastic wrap and refrigerate.

Hot Artichoke Dip

Preparation time: 10 minutes
Cooking time: 10–15 minutes
Serves: 6   Serving size: 1/4 cup

This wonderfully tangy dip leaves the mayonnaise-laden original far behind. The key: use the best Parmesan cheese you can find. Skip the pre-grated stuff, buy a wedge of imported Parmegiano-Reggiano and grate it yourself—it makes all the difference.

1	14-oz can artichoke hearts, drained
1	cup freshly grated Parmesan cheese
3	Tbsp lite mayonnaise
1	clove garlic, minced
1	Tbsp fresh lemon juice
	Pinch paprika
2	Tbsp minced onion
1/4	tsp seasoned salt
	Ground black pepper to taste

1. Preheat the oven to 400°F. Reserve 1 Tbsp of the cheese and set aside.

2. In a food processor or blender, combine the artichokes, the remaining cheese, the mayonnaise, garlic, lemon juice, and paprika; pulse until smooth. Stir in the onion and season with salt and pepper.

3. Spread the mixture into a small (2-cup) shallow baking dish and sprinkle with the reserved 1 Tbsp cheese. Bake until lightly browned and warmed through, about 10–15 minutes. Serve warm.

Exchanges
1 Lean Meat
1 Vegetable
1 Fat

Calories 112
   Calories from Fat . . 68
Total Fat . . . . 8 g
   Saturated Fat . . . . . . 3 g
Cholesterol . . . . 16 mg
Sodium . . . . 385 mg
Carbohydrate . . . . 5 g
   Dietary Fiber . . . . . . 1 g
   Sugars . . . . 2 g
Protein . . . . 7 g

Hummus

Preparation time: 5 minutes
Cooking time: none
Serves: 6   Serving size: 1/4 cup

In a Middle Eastern restaurant, this popular sesame dip usually comes with lots of warmed pita breads for dipping, and a pool of fruity olive oil on top. Just eliminating the oil pool saved a lot of fat and calories, as did cutting the amount of tahini (sesame paste) usually called for. We compensated by using a little toasted sesame oil, which delivers a lot of sesame flavor in a small drizzle. Try serving hummus with cut-up carrots and bell peppers for dipping.

1	15-oz can chickpeas (garbanzo beans), drained and rinsed
1/4	cup fresh lemon juice
2	Tbsp fat-free sour cream
1	Tbsp extra-virgin olive oil
1	Tbsp tahini
1–2	cloves garlic, minced
1/2	tsp toasted sesame oil
1/2	tsp ground cumin
1/4	tsp paprika
	Chopped flat-leaf (Italian) parsley, for garnish

In a food processor or blender, process the chickpeas, lemon juice, sour cream, olive oil, tahini, garlic, sesame oil, cumin, and paprika until smooth, adding 1 to 3 Tbsp of water as needed to obtain a creamy consistency. Garnish with the parsley and serve.

Exchanges
1 Starch
1 Fat

Calories 131
    Calories from Fat . . 48
Total Fat . . . . 5 g
    Saturated Fat . . . . . . 1 g
Cholesterol . . . . 0 mg
Sodium . . . . 87 mg
Carbohydrate . . . . . . 17 g
    Dietary Fiber . . . . . . 4 g
    Sugars . . . . 3 g
Protein . . . . 5 g

The hummus can be refrigerated, covered, for up to 2 days; let warm to room temperature before serving.

Nachos

Preparation time: 15 minutes
Cooking time: 3 minutes
Serves: 6   Serving size: 3/4 cup

The secret to lighter nachos? Look for low-fat tortilla chips with only 2 grams of fat per serving, then focus on adding flavorful vegetables rather than extra cheese. Green chiles, tomatoes, green onions, and jalapeño peppers give these appetizers their pizzazz.

  4 cups low-fat baked tortilla chips
  1 cup grated extra-sharp cheddar cheese
  2 Tbsp canned chopped green chiles
1/2 medium tomato, finely chopped
1/4 cup sliced pitted black olives
  1 green onion, finely chopped
  2 Tbsp chopped cilantro
1–2 pickled jalapeño peppers, sliced (optional)

1. Preheat the oven to 400°F. Spray a large heatproof platter or baking sheet with nonstick cooking spray.

2. Scatter the tortilla chips evenly over the platter. Sprinkle them evenly with the cheese and green chiles and broil until the cheese melts, 2 to 3 minutes.

3. Top the nachos with the chopped tomato, olives, onion, cilantro, and the jalapeño peppers, if using. Serve immediately.

Exchanges

1 Starch
1 Lean Meat
1 Fat

Calories 172
  Calories from Fat . . 79
Total Fat . . . . 9 g
  Saturated Fat . . . . . . 4 g
Cholesterol . . . . 20 mg
Sodium . . . . 319 mg
Carbohydrate . . . . . . 18 g
  Dietary Fiber . . . . . . 3 g
  Sugars . . . . 1 g
Protein . . . . 7 g

Quesadillas

Preparation time: 15 minutes
Cooking time: 10 minutes
Serves: 8   Serving size: 2 wedges

This super-simple appetizer is even faster if you have a pancake griddle; simply preheat, spray with nonstick cooking spray, and prepare all the quesadillas at once. Trim the fat even further by replacing the traditional cheeses with a reduced-fat jack cheese spiked with pepper.

- 1 cup shredded Mexican Chihuahua, Monterey Jack, Pepper Jack, or brick cheese
- 1 green onion, minced
- 1–3 Tbsp canned chopped green chiles (to taste)
- 4 8-inch flour tortillas
- Chunky salsa, for topping or dip

1. In a medium bowl, toss together the cheese, green onion, and chiles; set aside.

2. Spray a medium skillet with nonstick cooking spray and place over medium heat. When hot, add 1 tortilla and sprinkle it with one-fourth of the cheese mixture. When the cheese begins to melt, about 1 minute, fold the tortilla in half. Continue cooking until lightly browned and crisp on both sides, about 1 minute. Transfer to a cutting board. Repeat with the remaining tortillas and filling.

3. Cut into 4 wedges with a knife or pizza cutter and serve immediately with the salsa.

Exchanges

1 Starch
1 Fat

Calories 134
   Calories from Fat . . 55
Total Fat . . . . 6 g
   Saturated Fat . . . . . . 3 g
Cholesterol . . . . 12 mg
Sodium . . . . 211 mg
Carbohydrate . . . . . . 14 g
   Dietary Fiber . . . . . . 1 g
   Sugars . . . . 1 g
Protein . . . . 6 g

Spinach Dip

Preparation time: 10 minutes
Chilling time: 1 hour
Serves: 12   Serving size: 1/4 cup

This recipe calls for a vegetable snack mix found in the produce section of most major supermarkets. It's a medley of dehydrated vegetables—tiny bits of carrots, peas, corn, and dried tomatoes—intended for snacking. It adds color to the dip, but if you can't find it, don't worry—the recipe will work fine without it!

- 3/4 cup fat-free cottage cheese
- 1/4 cup reduced-fat brick-style cream cheese
- 2 Tbsp lite mayonnaise
- 1 10-oz package frozen spinach, thawed and squeezed dry
- 1 8-oz can water chestnuts, drained and finely chopped
- 1/2 cup dried vegetable snack mix, optional (not included in nutrient analysis)
- 2 green onions, white and green parts, finely chopped
- 2 Tbsp chopped fresh dill (or 1 Tbsp dried)
- 1/2 tsp dry mustard
- 1 small clove garlic, minced

1. In a food processor or blender, puree the cottage cheese, cream cheese, and mayonnaise until smooth.

2. In a medium bowl, combine the cottage cheese mixture with the spinach, water chestnuts, vegetable mix, green onions, dill, mustard, and garlic. Cover and refrigerate at least 1 hour to blend flavors. (The dip can be stored this way for up to 24 hours.)

Exchanges
1 Vegetable
1/2 Fat

Calories	45
Calories from Fat . .	17
Total Fat	2 g
Saturated Fat	1 g
Cholesterol	5 mg
Sodium	109 mg
Carbohydrate	4 g
Dietary Fiber	1 g
Sugars	2 g
Protein	3 g

Tortilla Chips

Preparation time: 10 minutes
Cooking time: 20 minutes
Serves: 6   Serving size: 8 chips

Making your own tortilla chips is not difficult. This recipe uses corn tortillas. Tortilla chips can be teamed up with the Chili Con Queso on page 91, or served with salsa or fat-free sour cream and fresh chopped tomatoes. Unused chips can be stored in an airtight container for up to 2 days.

> 1/2 tsp sweet Hungarian or regular paprika
> 1/2 tsp grated Parmesan cheese
>   2 Tbsp olive oil
>   6 6-inch corn tortillas

1. Place one oven rack on the lowest rung and another in the middle. Place a large flat pan on the lowest rack; pull out the rack halfway and fill the pan with 1 inch of hot water. Preheat the oven to 325°F.

2. Spray a baking sheet with nonstick cooking spray. In a small bowl, combine the paprika and cheese; set aside.

3. Pour the oil into a small bowl. Using a pastry brush, brush the tortillas on both sides with the oil.

4. Using a pizza cutter or a very sharp knife, cut each tortilla into 8 wedges. Arrange on the prepared baking sheet. Place the sheet on the middle rack and bake for 10 minutes; flip the wedges and bake 10 minutes longer. Sprinkle lightly with the paprika/cheese mixture.

Exchanges
1 Starch
1/2 Fat

Calories 95
  Calories from Fat . . 43
Total Fat . . . . 5 g
  Saturated Fat . . . . . . 1 g
Cholesterol . . . . 0 mg
Sodium . . . . 46 mg
Carbohydrate . . . . . . 12 g
  Dietary Fiber . . . . . . 1 g
  Sugars . . . . 0 g
Protein . . . . 2 g

The pan of water in the oven adds extra moisture so the chips don't become brittle. After baking the chips, the pan of water will be quite hot, so handle with hot pads or wait until it is cool to remove it. If you can find rich, complex Hungarian paprika, store it in the refrigerator—its flavor fades quickly.

Sauces, Gravies, & Dressings

*R*ecipes

Basic Vinaigrette Dressing

Preparation time: 5 minutes
Cooking time: none
Serves: 8   Serving size: 1 Tbsp

Substitute whichever herbs strike your fancy—say, thyme, basil, oregano, or tarragon—and this piquant, all-purpose dressing will take on a whole new character. It will last in the refrigerator about 1 week; shake well before using.

1   small clove garlic, minced
     Pinch salt
2   Tbsp red wine vinegar
2   tsp Dijon mustard
1/4 tsp fresh marjoram, or 1/8 tsp dried
     Ground black pepper to taste
1/4 cup low-sodium chicken broth
2   Tbsp extra-virgin olive oil

1. In a mortar and pestle (or a small bowl with a small spoon), mash the garlic and salt together into a paste.

2. In a small jar with a tight-fitting lid, combine the mashed garlic, vinegar, mustard, marjoram, and pepper; shake to blend. Add the broth and oil and shake until smooth.

Exchanges
1/2 Fat

Calories 30
  Calories from Fat . . 28
Total Fat . . . . 3 g
  Saturated Fat . . . . . . 1 g
Cholesterol . . . . 0 mg
Sodium . . . . 54 mg
Carbohydrate . . . . 1 g
  Dietary Fiber . . . . . . 0 g
  Sugars . . . . 0 g
Protein . . . . 0 g

Barbecue Sauce

Preparation time: 5 minutes
Cooking time: 5 minutes
Serves: 12   Serving size: 1 Tbsp

In our version of the popular Kansas City-style sauce, complex flavors replace a lot of the sugar. The flavors are highly concentrated, so you don't need to use as much as the bottled stuff. The recipe makes enough for a large chicken, two pork tenderloins, or 2 lb of beef steaks. Brush it on poultry or meats about 10 minutes before they're done on the grill; any longer than that and the sauce will burn. The recipe easily doubles; extra sauce will keep, covered, in the refrigerator up to 2 weeks.

3/4 cup ketchup
  1 Tbsp dark brown sugar
  1 Tbsp chili powder
  1 Tbsp cider vinegar
  1 Tbsp canola oil
  1 Tbsp hoisin sauce
  1 tsp onion powder
  1 tsp dry mustard
1/2 tsp Worcestershire sauce
  1 clove garlic, minced

In a small saucepan, combine all the ingredients. Bring to a boil and simmer, stirring as needed, until slightly thickened, 5 minutes. Let cool.

Exchanges
1/2 Carbohydrate

Calories 35
　Calories from Fat . . 12
Total Fat . . . . 1 g
　Saturated Fat . . . . . . 0 g
Cholesterol . . . . 0 mg
Sodium . . . . 214 mg
Carbohydrate . . . . 6 g
　Dietary Fiber . . . . . . 0 g
　Sugars . . . . 3 g
Protein . . . . 0 g

Hoisin sauce, a slightly sweet, fermented black bean sauce, can be found in the Asian foods section of most supermarkets and in Asian markets.

Caesar Dressing

Preparation time: 10 minutes
Cooking time: none
Serves: 8   Serving size: 1 Tbsp

Most of us have a love-hate relationship with Caesar dressing—love the flavor, hate the high fat content and the raw egg. This easy version eliminates all the negatives, deliciously. It will keep in the refrigerator up to 2 days, but each day the garlic will become a little more powerful. If you won't be using it immediately, use a half clove of garlic instead.

1/4	cup fat-free cottage cheese
1	clove garlic, minced
2	Tbsp grated Parmesan cheese
2	Tbsp lemon juice
2	Tbsp lite mayonnaise
1	tsp anchovy paste (optional)
1/2	tsp Dijon mustard

In a food processor or blender, puree the cottage cheese and garlic until smooth. Add the Parmesan cheese, the lemon juice, mayonnaise, anchovy paste if using, and the mustard; pulse until smooth. Let stand 10 minutes to allow flavors to blend.

Exchanges
1/2 Fat

Calories 27	
Calories from Fat . . 16	
Total Fat . . . . 2 g	
Saturated Fat . . . . . . 1 g	
Cholesterol . . . . 3 mg	
Sodium . . . . 96 mg	
Carbohydrate . . . . 1 g	
Dietary Fiber . . . . . . 0 g	
Sugars . . . . 1 g	
Protein . . . . 2 g	

Classic White Sauce (Béchamel)

Preparation time: 5 minutes
Cooking time: 20 minutes
Serves: 6   Serving size: 2 Tbsp

This delightful sauce has enough flavor that no one will ever notice the missing fat; use it as a base for creamed dishes. It follows the classic formula—flour heated in fat, with flavored milk stirred in—but with half the usual amount of fat. So, you need to be vigilant about whisking constantly, to prevent burning—low-fat sauces are less forgiving. If you're pressed for time or plan to use the sauce in an already highly flavored dish, try the Rush Hour White Sauce on p. 57.

1 1/4	cups low-fat (1%) milk
1/4	medium onion
1	bay leaf
3	whole cloves
1	Tbsp unsalted butter or nondiet margarine
2	Tbsp all-purpose flour
	Pinch salt
	Ground black pepper to taste
	Pinch dried thyme (optional)

1. In a small saucepan, combine the milk, onion, bay leaf, and cloves; bring to a simmer, reduce the heat, and cook just below simmering, stirring frequently, until the milk has absorbed the flavors, about 15 minutes. Remove from the heat. Remove the onion, bay leaf, and cloves; set aside.

2. In a medium saucepan, melt the butter. Add the flour, 1 Tbsp at a time, whisking constantly, until a smooth paste forms. It will get very thick, then loosen again; keep whisking until the mixture turns the color of light wood, about 1 1/2 minutes. Remove from the heat.

3. Very slowly, add the warmed milk mixture, whisking constantly to prevent lumps. (If some lumps form, just pour the sauce through a strainer.) Return to the heat and cook, whisking constantly, until the mixture bubbles and thickens, about 2 minutes. Season with salt, pepper, and thyme.

Exchanges
1/2 Starch
1/2 Fat

Calories 48
    Calories from Fat . . 22
Total Fat . . . . 2 g
    Saturated Fat . . . . . . 2 g
Cholesterol . . . . 7 mg
Sodium . . . . 38 mg
Carbohydrate . . . . 4 g
    Dietary Fiber . . . . . . 0 g
    Sugars . . . . 2 g
Protein . . . . 2 g

Fat-Free Brown Roux

Preparation time: 1 minute
Cooking time: 15 minutes
Serves: 16   Serving size: 1 Tbsp

At the heart of almost every Cajun and Creole dish is dark-brown roux, prepared by cooking equal parts flour and butter or oil sometimes as long as 20 minutes or more. The flour becomes deep brown and acquires a wonderful nutty flavor. Cookbook author Roy F. Guste Jr. devised this clever method of getting the browned roux taste without the fat. In this recipe, simply cook the flour in a dry pan until it darkens, then add it to the cooking liquids in the rest of the recipe. Prepare the roux ahead of time and store it in a tightly sealed container; it will keep up to 6 months. You can halve or double the recipe, too; just use a smaller or larger pan to compensate.

1 cup all-purpose flour

In a medium skillet over medium heat, cook the flour, stirring constantly with a wooden spoon to prevent burning. Within 7–8 minutes, the flour should begin to take on a pale tan color and nutty fragrance (blond roux); continue cooking and stirring until the flour takes on the color of light wood, about 15–18 minutes. Do not allow to brown (the roux will darken later, when it is added to liquid).

Exchanges
1/2 Starch

Calories 28
　Calories from Fat . . . 1
Total Fat . . . . 0 g
　Saturated Fat . . . . . . 0 g
Cholesterol . . . . 0 mg
Sodium . . . . 0 mg
Carbohydrate . . . . 6 g
　Dietary Fiber . . . . . . 0 g
　Sugars . . . . 0 g
Protein . . . . 1 g

Hollandaise Sauce

Preparation time: 10 minutes
Cooking time: 5 minutes
Serves: 8   Serving size: 2 Tbsp

This recipe uses the same technique as the mayonnaise recipe on the next page to make a lovely, light sauce that makes anything taste better—from a poached egg on toast to a platter of steamed broccoli. Make it often enough, and you just might eat more vegetables!

 1 Tbsp unsalted butter
3/4 cup low-fat (1%) buttermilk, divided
 2 tsp cornstarch
1/4 tsp dry mustard
1/4 tsp seasoned salt
    Pinch cayenne pepper
 1 egg
 2 Tbsp reduced-fat brick-style cream cheese
 1 tsp lemon juice

1. In a small skillet over medium-low heat, melt the butter until fragrant and golden brown, about 1 minute (watch for burning); remove from the heat and set aside.

2. In a medium saucepan, whisk 1/4 cup of the buttermilk with the cornstarch, mustard, salt, and pepper. Add the egg and the remaining buttermilk; whisk constantly over medium-low heat until the mixture begins to thicken, about 3 minutes. Add the cream cheese and continue whisking until smooth and heated through, 1 minute; remove from the heat. Whisk in the lemon juice and the reserved melted butter. Serve immediately, or cover and refrigerate for up to 2 days. To reheat, microwave on high about 45 seconds, stirring once.

Exchanges
1 Fat

Calories 43
  Calories from Fat . . 27
Total Fat . . . . 3 g
  Saturated Fat . . . . . . 2 g
Cholesterol . . . . 34 mg
Sodium . . . . 95 mg
Carbohydrate . . . . 2 g
  Dietary Fiber . . . . . . 0 g
  Sugars . . . . 1 g
Protein . . . . 2 g

Mayonnaise

Preparation time: 10 minutes
Cooking time: 4 minutes
Serves: 16   Serving size: 1 Tbsp

Sure, you can buy lite mayonnaise at the supermarket, but it often has added sugars and doesn't taste anything like homemade. When it's this easy to whip up your own version, it hardly makes sense to do anything else. This version calls for cooking the egg gently, removing salmonella risk, and it won't separate, either. The drawback: since it's thickened with cornstarch, it will thin out if combined with very acidic ingredients. Don't use it in a vinegary salad dressing, for example, or in acid-rich buttermilk Ranch dressing. Store it in the refrigerator for up to 4 days.

3/4	cup low-fat (1%) buttermilk
1	Tbsp cornstarch
1/2	tsp dry mustard
	Pinch seasoned salt
	Pinch cayenne pepper
1	egg, lightly beaten
2	Tbsp reduced-fat brick-style cream cheese
2	Tbsp fresh lemon juice

1. In a medium saucepan, whisk 1/4 cup of the buttermilk with the cornstarch, mustard, salt, and pepper. Add the egg and the remaining buttermilk; whisk constantly over medium-low heat until the mixture begins to thicken, about 3 minutes.

2. Add the cream cheese and continue whisking until smooth and heated through, 1 minute; remove from the heat. Whisk in the lemon juice.

3. Pour into a small bowl and cover with plastic wrap to prevent a skin from forming. Chill thoroughly.

Exchanges
Free Food

Calories	16
Calories from Fat	7
Total Fat	1 g
Saturated Fat	0 g
Cholesterol	15 mg
Sodium	27 mg
Carbohydrate	1 g
Dietary Fiber	0 g
Sugars	1 g
Protein	1 g

Meaty Tomato Sauce

Preparation time: 25 minutes
Cooking time: 2 hours
Serves: 12   Serving size: 3/4 cup

This is the kind of sauce Italian-American grandmas make, simmering on their stoves all Sunday afternoon. The key is to make meatballs first, then crumble them; that way you add the wonderful flavors of browned meat. (Cooking crumbled raw meat instead of meatballs doesn't allow for deep browning; the meat gives off so much water it steams before it browns.) Lean ground turkey makes a good substitute for beef, but it tends to lack flavor and can become dry. So, we've bumped up the traditional spices and used fresh bread crumbs instead of dried, for maximum tenderness.

2	oz crustless sturdy stale bread
1/2	pound lean ground turkey breast
1	egg
1/4	cup freshly grated Romano cheese
1/4	cup chopped fresh parsley
1	clove garlic, minced
1/2	tsp fresh ground black pepper
1	Tbsp extra-virgin olive oil
1	28-oz can diced tomatoes in juice
1	28-oz can crushed tomatoes

Exchanges
1 Very Lean Meat
2 Vegetable

Calories 88
  Calories from Fat . . 16
Total Fat . . . . 2 g
  Saturated Fat . . . . . . 1 g
Cholesterol . . . . 31 mg
Sodium . . . . 385 mg
Carbohydrate . . . . . . 11 g
  Dietary Fiber . . . . . . 2 g
  Sugars . . . . 6 g
Protein . . . . 8 g

1. To make fresh bread crumbs, grate the bread on the large holes in a box grater. You should have about 1 cup.

2. In a large bowl, lightly combine the turkey, bread crumbs, egg, cheese, parsley, garlic, and pepper. Let stand 10 minutes to moisten evenly. Shape the mixture into 12 meatballs.

3. In a large nonstick saucepan or deep skillet, heat the oil. Cook the meatballs, turning as needed, until well browned on all sides, 7–8 minutes. Transfer to a plate. Pour off all but 1 tsp of any oil remaining in the pan. Add the tomatoes and meatballs; bring to just below boiling. Reduce the heat to low; partially cover and simmer, stirring occasionally, until the meatballs are tender, at least 2 hours.

4. With a slotted spoon, remove the meatballs to a large bowl. Crumble with a wooden spoon (or, when cool enough to handle, with your hands), then return to the sauce and heat through.

Pan Gravy for Roasted Meats or Poultry

Preparation time: 20 minutes
Cooking time: 20 minutes
Serves: 6   Serving size: 2 Tbsp

Whether you're roasting chicken, turkey, or beef, this flavorful gravy will make it a treat. The rich flavors come from those browned bits that remain in the roasting pan; be sure to scrape the pan clean. Use a stock or broth appropriate to the roasted item: with roasted chicken or turkey, use chicken stock or broth; with beef, use beef stock or broth.

1/2–1 1/2 cups chicken or beef stock (preferably homemade), or low-sodium chicken or beef broth
1 Tbsp canola oil
2 Tbsp all-purpose flour
1 tsp fresh herbs (try thyme, marjoram, or sage), or 1/2 tsp dried
   Ground black pepper to taste

Exchanges
1/2 Fat

Calories	34
Calories from Fat	21
Total Fat	2 g
Saturated Fat	0 g
Cholesterol	0 mg
Sodium	80 mg
Carbohydrate	2 g
Dietary Fiber	0 g
Sugars	0 g
Protein	1 g

1. When the roasted meat/poultry is cooked, transfer it to a plate and keep warm. Pour off as much fat from the roasting pan as possible. Pour any pan juices that have accumulated into a fat separator; when the fat settles, pour it off and discard. Add enough stock or broth to the juices in the separator to make 1 1/2 cups.

2. Place the roasting pan on a burner over medium heat; add the broth mixture and cook, scraping up browned bits from the bottom of the pan, until the liquid is reduced to 1 cup. Remove from the heat and set aside.

3. In a medium saucepan, heat the oil. Add the flour, 1 Tbsp at a time, whisking constantly, until a smooth paste forms. It will get very thick, then loosen again; keep whisking until the mixture turns the color of light wood, about 1 1/2 minutes. Remove from the heat.

4. Very slowly, add the broth mixture, whisking constantly to prevent lumps. (If, despite your efforts, some lumps form, don't worry—just pour the sauce through a strainer.) Return to the heat and cook, whisking constantly, until the mixture bubbles and thickens, about 2 minutes. Season with herbs and pepper to taste.

Peanut Sauce

Preparation time: 5 minutes
Standing time: 1 hour
Serves: 8   Serving size: 2 Tbsp

This sauce is wonderful for dipping raw or steamed-crisp vegetables (try radishes, broccoli, and green beans). You can also serve it Indonesian satay style, alongside skewered strips of grilled lean beef or chicken breast. You can also use it to make sesame noodles: thin the sauce with an equal amount of water and toss with cold cooked noodles. You'll need about 2–3 Tbsp of the thinned sauce per 1/2 cup of noodles.

> 1/4 cup water
> 1/4 cup smooth natural peanut butter
> 1/4 cup fat-free refried beans
> 1 Tbsp soy sauce
> 1 Tbsp hoisin sauce
> 1 small clove garlic, minced
> 1/4 tsp dried red pepper flakes
> 2 Tbsp chopped cilantro, for garnish

1. In a food processor or blender, combine the water, peanut butter, beans, soy and hoisin sauces, garlic, and red pepper flakes; pulse until smooth. Add more water, a Tbsp at a time, until the sauce reaches dipping consistency.

2. Cover and let stand 1 hour to blend flavors. Sprinkle with the cilantro and serve. The sauce will keep, covered, in the refrigerator up to 4 days; it will thicken as it stands, but can be thinned with water.

Exchanges
1 Fat

Calories 58
  Calories from Fat . . 36
Total Fat . . . . 4 g
  Saturated Fat . . . . . . 1 g
Cholesterol . . . . 0 mg
Sodium . . . . 227 mg
Carbohydrate . . . . 4 g
  Dietary Fiber . . . . . . 1 g
  Sugars . . . . 1 g
Protein . . . . 3 g

Hoisin sauce, a slightly sweet, fermented black bean sauce, can be found in the Asian foods section of most supermarkets and in Asian markets.

Pesto

Preparation time: 20 minutes
Standing time: 1 hour
Serves: 4   Serving size: 2 Tbsp

There are probably too many variations on this Genovese classic these days, but few cut the fat as effortlessly as this one. In the traditional version, oil, nuts, and cheese give body to the sauce (along with a lot of fat and calories). We've borrowed a technique from Spanish cookery, in which stale bread is used as a thickener instead. The recipe will sauce 1 lb of pasta; try linguine or spaghetti.

    1 oz crustless sturdy stale bread, cubed
    2 cups packed basil leaves, washed and dried
    3 cloves garlic, coarsely chopped
    1 Tbsp extra-virgin olive oil
  1/2 cup freshly grated Parmesan cheese
    2 Tbsp toasted pine nuts
       Salt and pepper to taste

1. In a small bowl, combine the bread with enough water to nearly cover; let stand 10 minutes to soften. Squeeze out the water from the bread and set aside.

2. In a food processor or blender, combine the basil, garlic, and oil; process until finely chopped. Add the softened bread, 1/4 cup water, cheese, and pine nuts; process until nearly smooth, about 30 seconds. Season with salt and pepper. Let stand at room temperature at least 1 hour to blend flavors. Refrigerate, covered, for up to 1 day; bring to room temperature before using.

Exchanges
1/2 Carbohydrate
2 Fat

Calories 140
　Calories from Fat . . 91
Total Fat . . . . 10 g
　Saturated Fat . . . . . . 4 g
Cholesterol . . . . 14 mg
Sodium . . . . 280 mg
Carbohydrate . . . . . . 6 g
　Dietary Fiber . . . . . . 1 g
　Sugars . . . . 2 g
Protein . . . . 9 g

Ranch Dressing

Preparation time: 10 minutes
Chilling time: 10 minutes
Serves: 8   Serving size: 1 Tbsp

Created at Santa Barbara's Hidden Valley Guest Ranch in California, ranch dressing has been a favorite since the '50s. Our version is equivalent to the low-fat commercially prepared version, but tastes so much better, thanks to fresh herbs. When shopping for lite mayonnaise, compare labels; some are much lower in carbohydrate than others. Store in the refrigerator for up to 2 days; shake well before using. The recipe can easily be halved.

1	small clove garlic, minced
	Pinch salt
1/3	cup low-fat (1%) buttermilk
1/4	cup lite mayonnaise
1	tsp fresh lime juice
2	tsp snipped fresh chives
1	tsp minced fresh parsley

1. In a mortar and pestle (or a small bowl with a small spoon), mash the garlic and salt together to a paste.

2. In a small jar with a tight-fitting lid, add the buttermilk, mayonnaise, lime juice, chives, parsley, and the mashed garlic; shake well to blend. Refrigerate at least 10 minutes to allow flavors to blend.

Exchanges
1/2 Fat

Calories 30
    Calories from Fat . . 23
Total Fat . . . . 3 g
    Saturated Fat . . . . . . 0 g
Cholesterol . . . . 3 mg
Sodium . . . . 216 mg
Carbohydrate . . . . 1 g
    Dietary Fiber . . . . . . 0 g
    Sugars . . . . 1 g
Protein . . . . 0 g

Rush Hour White Sauce

Preparation time: 5 minutes
Cooking time: 5 minutes
Serves: 6   Serving size: 2 Tbsp

This quick white sauce works best as a base to add to creamed dishes; as a gravy, it may be a little plain. Key to success: instant-mixing flour, such as Wondra™, which doesn't need to be cooked before it is combined with the milk.

1	Tbsp unsalted butter or nondiet margarine
1 1/4	cups low-fat (1%) milk
2	Tbsp instant-mixing flour
1/4	tsp onion powder
	Pinch nutmeg

1. In a small saucepan over medium heat, melt the butter and continue cooking, stirring constantly, until it becomes golden brown and fragrant, about 1 minute (watch for burning). Remove from the heat and let cool slightly.

2. Whisk in the milk, flour, onion powder, and nutmeg; return to the heat and cook, whisking constantly, until thickened, about 3 minutes.

Exchanges
1/2 Starch
1/2 Fat

Calories	48
Calories from Fat	22
Total Fat	2 g
Saturated Fat	2 g
Cholesterol	7 mg
Sodium	26 mg
Carbohydrate	4 g
Dietary Fiber	0 g
Sugars	2 g
Protein	2 g

Strawberry Sauce

Preparation time: 5 minutes
Cooking time: none
Serves: 16   Serving size: 2 Tbsp

This versatile strawberry sauce keeps for several days in the refrigerator. Use over French toast, angel food cake, or waffles. The sauce will keep for several days if stored in a tightly covered container in the refrigerator.

- 1 lb frozen whole unsweetened strawberries, thawed
- 2 Tbsp granulated sugar
- 2 Tbsp fresh lemon juice

In a food processor or blender, process the strawberries, sugar, and lemon juice until smooth, about 1–2 minutes. If desired, strain the sauce through a cheesecloth, lined colander, or small sieve to remove strawberry seeds.

Exchanges
Free Food

Calories 16
  Calories from Fat . . . 0
Total Fat . . . . 0 g
  Saturated Fat . . . . . . 0 g
Cholesterol . . . . 0 mg
Sodium . . . . 1 mg
Carbohydrate . . . . 4 g
  Dietary Fiber . . . . . . 1 g
  Sugars . . . . 4 g
Protein . . . . 0 g

Sweet and Sour Curry Sauce

Preparation time: 5 minutes
Cooling time: 2 hours
Serves: 18   Serving size: 1 Tbsp

This sauce is good for dipping bite-size morsels of chicken or serving with roasted meats or boiled eggs. The curry will give it a flavor all its own.

1/2	cup fat-free sour cream
1/4	cup fat-free mayonnaise
2	Tbsp fresh lemon juice
1	Tbsp minced onion
2	tsp granulated sugar
1 1/2	tsp curry powder
1/4	tsp hot red pepper sauce

1. In a small bowl, whisk together the sour cream, mayonnaise, lemon juice, onion, sugar, curry powder, and hot sauce until smooth, 1–2 minutes.

2. Refrigerate at least 2 hours before serving.

Exchanges
Free Food

Calories	9
Calories from Fat	0
Total Fat	0 g
Saturated Fat	0 g
Cholesterol	0 mg
Sodium	32 mg
Carbohydrate	2 g
Dietary Fiber	0 g
Sugars	1 g
Protein	0 g

Curry comes in many exotic flavors, many more than the standard curry powder most cooks have in their spice racks. If you are new to curry, try the standard powder; then begin to experiment with the wide range of other curries that give entirely different tastes and colors. You may need to go to a specialty grocery store or spice store to find them.

Sweet and Sour Sauce

Preparation time: 5 minutes
Cooking time: none
Serves: 16   Serving size: 1 Tbsp

This sweet and sour sauce is easy and tangy. It is made with prepared mango chutney—sometimes called Major Grey's chutney—found near the ketchup in the grocery store. Although it contains no fat, it is high in carbohydrate, so take a tablespoon and stretch it a long way. Use it as a spread for sandwiches (great with roasted turkey or chicken breast), to add zing to a mayonnaise-based potato or chicken/turkey salad, or as a dip for the Herbed Chicken Bites (p. 72) or boiled shrimp.

> 1 9-oz bottle prepared mango chutney
> 3 Tbsp red wine vinegar
> 1 Tbsp canola oil
> 1 Tbsp prepared yellow mustard
> 1 Tbsp ketchup

In a food processor or blender, pulse the chutney, vinegar, 3 Tbsp water, oil, mustard, and ketchup until smooth.

Exchanges
1 Carbohydrate

Calories 59
   Calories from Fat . . . 8
Total Fat . . . . 1 g
   Saturated Fat . . . . . . 0 g
Cholesterol . . . . 0 mg
Sodium . . . . 161 mg
Carbohydrate . . . . . . 12 g
   Dietary Fiber . . . . . . 0 g
   Sugars . . . . 8 g
Protein . . . . 0 g

Once you make this sauce, chill it or use it immediately. Cover and refrigerate any leftovers for up to 1 week.

Tartar Sauce

Preparation time: 10 minutes
Chilling time: 10 minutes
Serves: 6   Serving size: 2 Tbsp

Make this once yourself, and you'll never turn to the bottled stuff again. You'll save fat and sodium, to boot. If you use our homemade Mayonnaise, be sure to use the sauce within an hour. Because of the acidity of the added ingredients, it will lose its thickness within a few hours. (If you want to make the sauce well ahead of time, just opt for commercial reduced-fat mayonnaise; it will last in the refrigerator about 2 days.) The recipe can easily be halved.

1/2 cup Mayonnaise (p. 51) or commercially prepared reduced-fat mayonnaise
2 Tbsp finely diced peeled cucumber
1 Tbsp finely diced dill pickles (1/2 oz)
1 Tbsp minced green onion
1 tsp capers

In a small bowl, combine all ingredients. Refrigerate 10 minutes to allow flavors to blend.

Exchanges

(for homemade mayonnaise)
1/2 Fat

Calories	23
Calories from Fat	10
Total Fat	1 g
Saturated Fat	1 g
Cholesterol	20 mg
Sodium	108 mg
Carbohydrate	2 g
Dietary Fiber	0 g
Sugars	1 g
Protein	1 g

Exchanges

(for store mayonnaise)
1 1/2 Fat

Calories	68
Calories from Fat	60
Total Fat	7 g
Saturated Fat	1 g
Cholesterol	7 mg
Sodium	233 mg
Carbohydrate	2 g
Dietary Fiber	0 g
Sugars	0 g
Protein	0 g

Thousand Island Dressing

Preparation time: 10 minutes
Chilling time: 10 minutes
Serves: 8   Serving size: 1 Tbsp

The perfect topping for a Reuben sandwich or crisp salad, Thousand Island dressing is a delight—but the bottled low-fat stuff is sadly lacking in flavor. Making your own dressing is easy! If you use our homemade Mayonnaise, be sure to use the sauce within an hour. Because of the acidity of the added ingredients, it will lose its thickness within a few hours. (If you want to make the sauce well ahead of time, just opt for commercial reduced-fat mayonnaise; it will last in the refrigerator about 2 days.) The recipe can easily be halved.

> 1/2 cup Mayonnaise (p. 51) or commercially prepared reduced-fat mayonnaise
> 4 tsp chili sauce or ketchup
> 2 tsp minced dill or half-sour pickles
> 1 tsp minced onion
> 1 tsp minced fresh parsley

In a small bowl, combine all ingredients. Refrigerate 10 minutes to allow flavors to blend.

Exchanges
(using homemade
   mayonnaise)
Free Food

Calories 19
   Calories from Fat . . . 7
Total Fat . . . . 1 g
   Saturated Fat . . . . . . 0 g
Cholesterol . . . . 15 mg
Sodium . . . . 75 mg
Carbohydrate . . . . 2 g
   Dietary Fiber . . . . . . 0 g
   Sugars . . . . 1 g
Protein . . . . 1 g

Yogurt Cheese

Preparation time: 1 minute
Chilling time: 8 hours
Serves: 8   Serving size: 2 Tbsp

Everyone should have a supply of this versatile spread in their refrigerators. It can be used almost anywhere you'd use cream cheese or sour cream: spread it on toast or bagels, dab some on a baked potato, stir it with some chopped herbs and a little reduced-fat mayonnaise to make a delightful dip. When buying yogurt, check labels and avoid any that contain starches or gums, as they will affect the texture.

3 cups fat-free plain yogurt

Spoon the yogurt into a coffee filter or cheesecloth-lined strainer; place over a large bowl. Cover with plastic wrap and refrigerate at least 8 hours or overnight. Discard the liquid.

Exchanges
Free Food

Calories 16
   Calories from Fat . . . 0
Total Fat . . . . 0 g
   Saturated Fat . . . . . . 0 g
Cholesterol . . . . 0 mg
Sodium . . . . 20 mg
Carbohydrate . . . . 2 g
   Dietary Fiber . . . . . . 0 g
   Sugars . . . . 1 g
Protein . . . . 2 g

*F*aux Fried Foods

Recipes

Better Burgers

Preparation time: 5 minutes
Cooking time: 12 minutes
Serves: 4   Serving size: 1 burger

This better burger is made with ground turkey breast. Serve it with a tomato slice and spinach on an English muffin and you've got a great meal with extra nutrients.

- 1 lb ground lean turkey breast
- 1/4 small onion, minced
- 2 Tbsp chopped fresh parsley
- 1/4 tsp dried basil
- 1/4 tsp dried oregano
- 1/4 tsp salt
- 1/8 tsp ground white pepper
- 1 egg, lightly beaten
- 1 Tbsp all-purpose flour
- 2 Tbsp grated Parmesan cheese

1. In a medium bowl, combine the turkey, onion, parsley, basil, oregano, salt, and pepper until well blended. With a fork, blend in the egg and flour. Shape the mixture into 4 burgers, about 1/2 inch thick.

2. Spray a medium skillet with nonstick cooking spray; heat. Cook the burgers, turning occasionally until fully cooked, about 5–7 minutes on each side. Sprinkle each burger with 1/2 Tbsp cheese before serving.

Exchanges
4 Very Lean Meat
1/2 Fat

Calories	169
Calories from Fat	45
Total Fat	5 g
Saturated Fat	1 g
Cholesterol	114 mg
Sodium	277 mg
Carbohydrate	2 g
Dietary Fiber	0 g
Sugars	1 g
Protein	28 g

Crab Cakes

Preparation time: 5 minutes
Cooking time: 10 minutes
Serves: 8   Serving size: 1 cake

Crab cakes are an eastern regional favorite. The ingredients are very simple and preparation time is minimal. You can usually find fresh crab meat at the seafood counter in your market, but if you must use canned, drain it first. The Old Bay Seasoning used in this recipe can be found in the spice section or at the seafood counter. If you can't find it, use 1/2 tsp sweet paprika and increase the thyme to 3/4 tsp.

1	lb snow or lump crab meat
2	slices white bread, made into crumbs
2	eggs, slightly beaten
1/2	red bell pepper, finely chopped
2	Tbsp all-purpose flour
2	Tbsp minced fresh parsley
2	Tbsp fresh lemon juice
1	Tbsp fat-free mayonnaise
1	tsp Old Bay Seasoning
1/2	tsp dried thyme
1/2	tsp cayenne pepper
2	tsp olive oil

1. Pick through the crab meat to remove any shells. In a medium bowl, combine the crab, bread crumbs, eggs, pepper, flour, parsley, lemon juice, mayonnaise, Old Bay Seasoning, thyme, and cayenne pepper until blended. Shape the mixture into 8 round cakes.

2. In a medium skillet, heat the oil. Add the cakes and brown on each side, about 1–2 minutes. Continue cooking, covered, over medium-low heat, turning occasionally until fully cooked, about 4–5 minutes on each side.

Exchanges
1/2 Starch
2 Very Lean Meat

Calories 106
    Calories from Fat . . 28
Total Fat . . . . 3 g
    Saturated Fat . . . . . . 1 g
Cholesterol . . . . 87 mg
Sodium . . . . 313 mg
Carbohydrate . . . . 7 g
    Dietary Fiber . . . . . . 1 g
    Sugars . . . . 1 g
Protein . . . . 12 g

King crab claw meat can be substituted for the snow crab, but may be more expensive. Imitation crab can be used as a lower-sodium choice, but results in a slightly different flavor.

Fish Sticks

Preparation time: 10 minutes
Cooking time: 20–25 minutes
Serves: 8   Serving size: 2 sticks

Even fish haters and the pickiest kids can't turn down these crisp, puffed morsels of fish. Pollack is the ideal choice, since it holds together best when cooked, though cod or haddock also work well. Serve the sticks with Tartar Sauce (p. 61) and a quick slaw of packaged shredded cabbage tossed with a little low-fat Italian dressing.

1 Tbsp canola oil
1 egg
2/3 cup instant potato flakes
2 lb firm white fish fillets, such as pollack, cod, or haddock, cut into 16 4-inch-long, 1/2-inch-wide strips
Pinch seasoned salt
Pinch cayenne pepper

1. Preheat the oven to 400°F.

2. Grease a baking sheet with the oil. Beat the egg in a small shallow bowl, and pour the potato flakes in a pie plate or shallow bowl.

3. One at a time, dip the fish fillets in the egg mixture, then dredge in the potato flakes, pressing with your fingers to help the flakes adhere. Place the fish on the prepared baking sheet.

4. Sprinkle the fish with the seasoned salt and cayenne pepper. Bake, turning once, until puffy and golden, 20–25 minutes.

Exchanges
3 Very Lean Meat

Calories 126
  Calories from Fat . . 24
Total Fat . . . . 3 g
  Saturated Fat . . . . . . 0 g
Cholesterol . . . . 75 mg
Sodium . . . . 78 mg
Carbohydrate . . . . 3 g
  Dietary Fiber . . . . . . 0 g
  Sugars . . . . 0 g
Protein . . . . 21 g

French Fries

Preparation time: 10 minutes
Chilling time: 24 hours
Cooking time: 20–25 minutes
Serves: 6   Serving size: 10 fries

You've probably made oven fries before, but were disappointed in the results, because there wasn't enough fat to really brown and crisp the fries. But you can get around that by refrigerating the unpeeled potatoes at least 1 day and up to 2 days ahead. Chilling them makes some of their starch convert to sugar, so they brown more in the oven. You'll also like using lemon pepper instead of salt; its acidic tang creates a sense of saltiness in the mouth.

> 1 1/2 lb Idaho potatoes, chilled and peeled
> 1 Tbsp vegetable oil
> Lemon pepper seasoning, to taste

1. Preheat the oven to 425°F.

2. Slice the potatoes into 1/4-inch-wide, 1/2-inch-thick strips. Rinse them in several changes of cold water, then blot dry with paper towels.

3. In a medium bowl, toss the potatoes with the oil, coating them evenly. Arrange the potatoes in a single layer on 2 baking sheets. Bake, turning occasionally, until evenly browned and crisp, about 20–25 minutes. Sprinkle with lemon pepper and serve immediately.

Exchanges

1 Starch

Calories 88
  Calories from Fat . . 22
Total Fat . . . . 2 g
  Saturated Fat . . . . . . 0 g
Cholesterol . . . . 0 mg
Sodium . . . . 5 mg
Carbohydrate . . . . . . 15 g
  Dietary Fiber . . . . . . 1 g
  Sugars . . . . 1 g
Protein . . . . 2 g

Fried Rice

Preparation time: 20 minutes
Cooking time: 15 minutes
Serves: 6   Serving size: 1 cup

This is the classic version you get in most Chinese restaurants (with more veggies, less fat, and more flavor!), but you can vary the ingredients with what you have on hand. If you have leftover roasted chicken, turkey, or pork, use that instead of ham, or small scallops instead of the shrimp. The key to success is to make sure the cooked rice is thoroughly cold before you use it. Make it a day or two ahead if possible, and keep it covered in the refrigerator until you use it.

1	egg
1	egg white
1	Tbsp peanut oil
4	green onions, white and green parts, finely chopped
1/2	medium red bell pepper, chopped
1/2	medium green bell pepper, chopped
1	cup sliced mushrooms
2	oz lean ham, diced
2	cups cold cooked rice, stirred to separate the grains
1/2	lb cooked (or thawed frozen) small shrimp
1	cup bean sprouts
1/2	cup thawed frozen green peas
1	Tbsp soy sauce

Exchanges

1 Starch
2 Very Lean Meat
1 Vegetable

Calories 185
    Calories from Fat . . 39
Total Fat . . . . 4 g
    Saturated Fat . . . . . . 1 g
Cholesterol . . . . 114 mg
Sodium . . . . 415 mg
Carbohydrate . . . . . . 21 g
    Dietary Fiber . . . . . . 2 g
    Sugars . . . . 2 g
Protein . . . . 15 g

1. In a small bowl, whisk together the egg and egg white; set aside.

2. In a large skillet or wok, heat the oil. Add the green onions, red and green peppers, and mushrooms; stir-fry until the mushrooms have released and reabsorbed their juices, 5–8 minutes. Add the ham and cook until lightly browned, 2 minutes. Add the rice and stir-fry until heated through, about 1 minute.

3. Make a well in the center of the rice and pour in the egg mixture. Cook, stirring gently, until the eggs are barely firm, about 1 minute. Add the shrimp, bean sprouts, peas, and soy sauce; cook, tossing lightly, until the bean sprouts are tender, about 3 minutes. Serve immediately.

Herbed Chicken Bites

Preparation time: 10 minutes
Cooking time: 25–30 minutes
Serves: 5   Serving size: 5 pieces

Chicken Bites aren't just for kids! Adults will like the taste of this baked version too. The chicken can easily be cut into small pieces if slightly frozen. You can do this ahead of time and leave in the refrigerator to fully thaw until you're ready to make the nuggets.

1/4	cup plain dried bread crumbs
2	Tbsp grated Parmesan cheese
1	Tbsp all-purpose flour
1	tsp dried oregano
1	tsp dried basil
1/8	tsp ground white pepper
2	Tbsp low-fat (1%) milk
1 1/4	lb boneless, skinless chicken breasts, cubed

1. Preheat the oven to 375°F. Line a baking sheet with parchment paper or spray with nonstick cooking spray.

2. In a quart-sized zippered plastic bag, add the bread crumbs, cheese, flour, oregano, basil, and pepper; shake to mix.

3. In a medium bowl, add the milk and chicken pieces, stirring to coat. Place 4–5 chicken pieces in the bag and shake gently until lightly coated. Place on the prepared baking sheet, then repeat with the remaining chicken.

4. Bake until golden brown, about 25–30 minutes.

Exchanges
1/2 Starch
4 Very Lean Meat

Calories 163
　Calories from Fat . . 23
Total Fat . . . . 3 g
　Saturated Fat . . . . . . 1 g
Cholesterol . . . . 66 mg
Sodium . . . . 158 mg
Carbohydrate . . . . 5 g
　Dietary Fiber . . . . . . 0 g
　Sugars . . . . 0 g
Protein . . . . 28 g

If you do not have a zippered bag, you can mix the crumb mixture in a bowl, add the chicken cubes 4–5 at a time, and stir to coat.

Oven-Fried Chicken

Preparation time: 10 minutes
Marinating time: 2 hours
Cooking time: 40 minutes
Serves: 7   Serving size: 1/7 recipe

This crispy-coated chicken comes out of the oven, not a deep-fat fryer. But just like fried chicken, it's delightful hot, warm, or cold. It's also juicy and tender, thanks to its buttermilk marinade. While you're baking the chicken, why not use the other oven rack to bake some thinly sliced carrots and chunks of potato? Just drizzle the vegetables with a little olive oil, sprinkle with pepper and thyme, and bake. They'll be ready when the chicken is!

1	3 1/2-lb chicken, cut into 7 pieces and skinned
1	cup low-fat (1%) buttermilk
2	Tbsp canola oil
3/4	cup cornflake crumbs
1	tsp dried thyme
1	tsp dried oregano
1/2	tsp fresh ground black pepper

1. In a gallon-size zippered plastic bag, combine the chicken and buttermilk. Seal the bag, squeezing out air; turn to coat the chicken. Refrigerate at least 2 hours and up to 8 hours, turning the bag occasionally. Drain the chicken and discard the buttermilk.

2. Preheat the oven to 400°F. Line a baking sheet with foil and coat with 1 Tbsp of the oil.

3. In a gallon-size zippered plastic bag, combine the cornflake crumbs, thyme, oregano, and pepper; shake well. Add the chicken, one piece at a time, and shake the bag to coat the chicken well. Place on the prepared baking sheet and drizzle evenly with the remaining oil. Bake until cooked through and the juices run clear when the chicken is pierced in the thickest part with a fork, 35–40 minutes.

Exchanges
1/2 Starch
3 Lean Meat

Calories 206
   Calories from Fat . . 77
Total Fat . . . . 9 g
   Saturated Fat . . . . . . 2 g
Cholesterol . . . . 65 mg
Sodium . . . . 168 mg
Carbohydrate . . . . 9 g
   Dietary Fiber . . . . . . 0 g
   Sugars . . . . 1 g
Protein . . . . 22 g

Sweet and Sour Pork

Preparation time: 15 minutes
Marinating time: 1 hour
Cooking time: 20 minutes
Serves: 6   Serving size: 1 cup

The Chinese-American take-out version, with its greasily breaded meat and candy-sweet sauce, is a mere shadow of the subtle, classic Cantonese dish. Our version is more faithful to the original; you'll love the difference. If you prefer, skinless turkey breast is a fine substitute for the pork.

1	Tbsp soy sauce
1	tsp rice wine vinegar
1	tsp granulated sugar
8	oz lean pork loin, trimmed of fat and cut into 1-inch cubes
1/4	cup water
1/4	cup cornstarch, divided
4	tsp peanut oil, divided
1	1/2-inch piece peeled gingerroot, minced
1	clove garlic, minced
1	green bell pepper, cut into 1-inch pieces
1	red bell pepper, cut into 1-inch pieces
1	small onion, cut into 1-inch cubes
1	8-oz can unsweetened pineapple chunks, drained
6	green onions, green part, cut into 1-inch pieces
2	Tbsp rice wine vinegar
1	Tbsp granulated sugar
1	Tbsp soy sauce

1. In a gallon-size zippered plastic bag, combine the soy sauce, vinegar, and sugar; add the pork. Seal the bag, squeezing out air; turn to coat the pork. Refrigerate about 1 hour, turning the bag occasionally. Drain, discarding the marinade.

2. In a small bowl, whisk together the water and 2 tsp of the cornstarch; set aside.

3. Sprinkle the remaining cornstarch onto a plate. One piece at a time, dredge the pork in the cornstarch, shaking off the excess, until coated on all sides. Discard any leftover cornstarch.

4. In a large nonstick skillet or wok, heat 2 tsp of the oil. Add the pork and stir-fry until lightly browned, about 5 minutes; transfer to a plate.

5. Return the skillet to the heat. Add 1 more tsp of the oil; heat. Add the ginger and garlic; stir-fry until fragrant, 1 minute, then add the green and red peppers and the onion. Continue cooking, stirring gently, until the peppers are tender, about 10 minutes; transfer to a plate and keep warm.

6. Return the skillet to the heat. Add the remaining tsp oil; heat. Stir-fry the pineapple and green onions until the pineapple is lightly browned, about 3 minutes. Stir in the reserved pork, the pepper-onion mixture, and the cornstarch mixture; cook, stirring as needed, until heated through and the sauce thickens, about 2 minutes. Stir in the vinegar, sugar, and soy sauce; cook, stirring gently as needed, until heated through, 1 minute.

Exchanges
1 Lean Meat
2 Vegetable
1/2 Fruit
1/2 Fat

Calories 140
  Calories from Fat . . 91
Total Fat . . . . 10 g
  Saturated Fat . . . . . . 4 g
Cholesterol . . . . 14 mg
Sodium . . . . 280 mg
Carbohydrate . . . . 6 g
  Dietary Fiber . . . . . . 1 g
  Sugars . . . . 2 g
Protein . . . . 9 g

Potato Pancakes

Preparation time: 5 minutes
Cooking time: 30 minutes
Serves: 4   Serving size: 2 pancakes

Think potato pancakes are time-consuming, greasy, and heavy? This version is light, flavorful, and best of all, easy. You can buy shredded hash brown potatoes in the dairy or frozen food aisles that make this recipe especially quick. Serve with salsa for extra zip.

2	eggs
1/4	medium onion, diced
2	Tbsp all-purpose flour
2	Tbsp fresh lemon juice
1/2	tsp salt
1/4	tsp ground white pepper
2	cups shredded hash brown potatoes, thawed (if frozen) and patted dry

1. In a medium bowl, beat the eggs well. Add the onion, flour, lemon juice, salt, and pepper and whisk until blended. Stir in the potatoes.

2. Spray a small nonstick skillet with nonstick cooking spray; heat. Drop heaping table-spoons of batter into the skillet. Cook until the edges of the pancakes appear formed, 3–4 minutes; flip and cook, 3–4 minutes longer, or until firm in the center. Remove and keep warm.

3. Repeat, spraying the skillet each time, until you make 8 pancakes.

Exchanges
1 Starch

Calories 89
   Calories from Fat . . 25
Total Fat . . . . 3 g
   Saturated Fat . . . . . . 1 g
Cholesterol . . . . 107 mg
Sodium . . . . 330 mg
Carbohydrate . . . . . . 11 g
   Dietary Fiber . . . . . . 1 g
   Sugars . . . . 1 g
Protein . . . . 4 g

If you prefer to use fresh potatoes, peel two medium potatoes, then shred directly into a bowl of cold water. Drain in a colander and rinse under cold running water. Squeeze the shredded potatoes in paper toweling to remove as much water as possible. Using fresh potatoes will extend the cooking time to 5–6 minutes per side.

Mom's Favorites

Recipes

Basic Quiche

Preparation time: 5 minutes
Cooking time: 50 minutes
Serves: 6   Serving size: 1/6 recipe

You can vary the cheese and vegetables in this custard-like egg dish to suit your taste or the season. Try sharp cheddar, Gruyère, or Swiss cheese for a variation. Other vegetables that work well include cooked drained spinach, sun-dried tomatoes, red bell peppers, and sliced zucchini.

1	recipe Buttery Pie Crust (p. 185)
3	eggs
3/4	cup low-fat (1%) milk
1/4	cup shredded part-skim mozzarella cheese
6	slices Canadian bacon, chopped into 1/4-inch pieces
1 1/2	cups sliced fresh mushrooms
1/4	tsp ground white pepper
1/8	tsp nutmeg
1/8	tsp dried thyme

1. Preheat the oven to 350°F. Prepare a deep 9-inch pie plate with pie crust as directed in the recipe.

2. In a medium bowl, with an electric mixer at medium speed, beat the eggs 1 minute. Stir in the milk, cheese, bacon, mushrooms, pepper, nutmeg, and thyme.

3. Pour into the prepared pie crust and bake until the top is firm and brown, about 50 minutes.

Exchanges

1 1/2 Starch
1 Medium-Fat Meat
2 Fat

Calories 290
  Calories from Fat . 147
Total Fat . . . . 16 g
  Saturated Fat . . . . . . 3 g
Cholesterol . . . . 124 mg
Sodium . . . . 386 mg
Carbohydrate . . . . . . 23 g
  Dietary Fiber . . . . . . 1 g
  Sugars . . . . 3 g
Protein . . . . 12 g

Basic Pot Roast

Preparation time: 25 minutes
Cooking time: 1 1/2 hours
Serves: 8   Serving size: 1 1/2 cups

This is probably one of the first, and best, one-pot meals. Make it on a day off or the weekend as it requires extra cooking time. It is very simple to put together, and the magic takes place while you are out of the kitchen. Although there are many ways to spice up this basic recipe, you will enjoy this version for its simplicity and fresh taste. The keys to the recipe are browning the meat and mixing the essence into the au jus, and cooking the vegetables just until they are tender.

2	lb boneless beef chuck arm roast, or similar cut, trimmed
1	Tbsp canola oil
1	medium onion, chopped
2	garlic cloves, minced
4 1/2	cups water, divided
2	bay leaves
1	tsp ground black pepper
6	medium potatoes, skins on, quartered
1	lb carrots, sliced 1/4 inch thick
5	stalks celery, cut into 1-inch pieces
3	Tbsp all-purpose flour

1. In a Dutch oven or large pot with a lid, heat the oil on medium high, then add the meat and brown on both sides so a crispy crust forms, about 5–8 minutes per side. Reduce the heat to medium low and add the onion and garlic; cook until the onion is translucent, about 3 minutes.

2. Transfer the beef to a plate; keep warm. Return the pan to the heat; add 2 cups water and cook, scraping up browned bits from the bottom of the pan. Return the beef to the pot, add the bay leaves and pepper, then cover and cook on low 1 hour, turning after 1/2 hour.

3. Add the potatoes on top of the meat and 2 more cups water. Cover and simmer 10 minutes. Add the carrots and celery, cover, and simmer until a fork can easily pierce a potato, about 15 minutes.

4. Remove the bay leaves and discard. Remove the meat to a cutting board and slice; arrange the slices in a large serving dish. With a slotted spoon remove the potatoes, carrots, and celery and place around meat in serving dish. Keep warm.

5. In a small bowl, combine the flour with 1/2 cup cold water until blended. Stir into remaining liquid in the pot. Cook, stirring constantly, over medium heat until thickened, about 3 minutes. Serve with the meat and vegetables.

Exchanges
2 Starch
3 Lean Meat
1 Vegetable

Calories 352
   Calories from Fat . . 84
Total Fat . . . . 9 g
   Saturated Fat . . . . . . 3 g
Cholesterol . . . . 93 mg
Sodium . . . . 110 mg
Carbohydrate . . . . . . 32 g
   Dietary Fiber . . . . . . 5 g
   Sugars . . . . 7 g
Protein . . . . 34 g

Boston Baked Beans

Preparation time: 10 minutes
Standing time: 8 hours
Cooking time: 5 hours
Serves: 16   Serving size: 1/2 cup

Grandma's beans were made with lard, brown sugar, molasses, and lots of spices. You won't find lard in this recipe, but you will find the same great flavor. If you've never used dried beans before, washing and soaking instructions are included. Making baked beans is not complicated, and it's more fun than just opening up a can!

1	lb dried navy beans
1	large onion, chopped
2	tsp salt
1	tomato, chopped
1/3	cup firmly packed dark brown sugar
3	Tbsp molasses
2	Tbsp cider vinegar
1	Tbsp ketchup
1	Tbsp ground ginger
1	tsp dry mustard
1/4	tsp ground white pepper

1. Place the beans in a strainer and sort through the beans to remove stones, discolored beans, or any other objects. Rinse with cold water until beans are clean, about 2 minutes.

2. In a large bowl, combine the beans, onion, salt, and enough water to cover them by 2 inches. Let stand 8 hours or overnight at room temperature; do not refrigerate.

3. Preheat the oven to 300°F.

4. In a strainer, drain and rinse the beans and onion. Place in a 4-quart saucepan and add the tomato, sugar, molasses, vinegar, ketchup, ginger, mustard, and pepper; stir until blended. Add enough water to cover the beans, about 2 cups. Cover and bake until bubbly and the beans are soft, 5 hours.

Exchanges
1 1/2 Starch

Calories 110
 Calories from Fat . . . 4
Total Fat . . . . 0 g
 Saturated Fat . . . . . . 0 g
Cholesterol . . . . 0 mg
Sodium . . . . 50 mg
Carbohydrate . . . . . . 21 g
 Dietary Fiber . . . . . . 4 g
 Sugars . . . . 4 g
Protein . . . . 6 g

Breakfast Strata

Preparation time: 10 minutes
Chilling time: 8 hours
Cooking time: 30 minutes
Serves: 6   Serving size: 1/6 recipe

When you think of breakfast strata, do layers of bread, cheese, eggs, bacon, and other high-fat ingredients come to mind? This unique strata limits the bread and fat and uses a spicy cheese to add zip. The strata is best made at least 8 hours ahead (or overnight) and refrigerated. In the morning, just bake—and eat!

> 3/4 cup egg substitute or 3 eggs
> 3/4 cup low-fat (1%) milk
>   3 slices day-old white bread, cubed
> 1/2 cup fresh spinach, finely chopped
> 1/2 cup shredded Pepper Jack cheese

1. Spray an 8-inch round pan with nonstick cooking spray.

2. In a medium bowl, whisk the eggs until frothy. Add the milk and bread. Let stand for 5 minutes. Add the spinach and cheese and stir to blend. Pour into the prepared pan. Cover and refrigerate 8 hours or overnight.

3. Preheat the oven to 350°F.

4. Bake the strata, uncovered, until the top is lightly browned, about 30 minutes. Serve hot or at room temperature.

Exchanges

1/2 Starch
1 Lean Meat

Calories 99
  Calories from Fat . . 32
Total Fat . . . . 4 g
  Saturated Fat . . . . . . 2 g
Cholesterol . . . . 10 mg
Sodium . . . . 209 mg
Carbohydrate . . . . 9 g
  Dietary Fiber . . . . . . 0 g
  Sugars . . . . 2 g
Protein . . . . 7 g

Top this great strata with diced tomatoes or sliced fruit to serve.

Candied Yams

Preparation time: 10 minutes
Cooking time: 1 hour 40 minutes
Serves: 9   Serving size: 1/2 cup

Sweet potatoes and yams are often mistaken for each other, although both are considered tuber vegetables to those who live in warm climates in South America, Asia, and the southern United States. The sweet potato is sweet and distinct in flavor. The yam has a less sweet taste and compliments a spicy or sweet dish. Feel free to use sweet potatoes instead of yams in this traditional Thanksgiving dish.

4   medium yams
    (about 2–2 1/2 pounds)
1/4   cup firmly packed dark
    brown sugar
1 1/2   tsp cinnamon
1/2   tsp ground cloves
1   Granny Smith apple, peeled
    and thinly sliced
3/4   cup apple cider
2   Tbsp stick margarine, cut
    into pea-size pieces

1. Preheat the oven to 350°F. Spray an 8 × 8-inch baking dish with nonstick cooking spray.

2. Place the yams on a baking sheet and bake until the skin feels soft to the touch, 60 minutes. Cool, peel, and slice into 1/8–1/4-inch rounds.

3. In a small bowl, whisk the sugar, cinnamon, and cloves.

4. In the baking dish, place half of the yams, then the apple slices, then half of the sugar mixture. Top with the remaining yams and sugar mixture. Pour the cider around the edges of the baking dish. Evenly scatter the margarine pieces on top.

5. Bake, covered, until bubbly and the yams are tender, about 40 minutes.

Exchanges
2 Starch

Calories 174
    Calories from Fat . . 25
Total Fat . . . . 3 g
    Saturated Fat . . . . . . 0 g
Cholesterol . . . . 0 mg
Sodium . . . . 39 mg
Carbohydrate . . . . . . 37 g
    Dietary Fiber . . . . . . 4 g
    Sugars . . . . 11 g
Protein . . . . 1 g

Since the yams need to cook for an hour before you make this recipe, you may want to prepare them a day or two in advance. Then just bake, cool, cover, and refrigerate them until you're ready to make the dish.

All tuber vegetables vary in final cooking times due to individual differences in their starch content. As they mature, the starch begins to break down, and the vegetable will require a slightly shorter cooking time.

Chicken Cacciatore

Preparation time: 20 minutes
Cooking time: 25 minutes
Serves: 6   Serving size: 1/6 recipe

This dish is always a favorite. It makes the kitchen smell good, has a delicious tomato taste, and is easy to prepare. Be sure to use juice-packed whole tomatoes without tomato puree for best flavor.

    2 Tbsp olive oil
    2 lb skinless, boneless chicken breasts
    2 red bell peppers, sliced
    1 large onion, chopped
    1 lb fresh mushrooms, sliced
 1–2 garlic cloves, minced
    1 28-oz can reduced-sodium whole tomatoes in juice
    2 tsp tomato paste
  1/4 cup dry white wine
    1 tsp dried basil or 3–4 fresh leaves

1. In a large nonstick skillet, heat the oil over medium-high heat.

2. Add the chicken breasts and sauté on both sides for a total of 6 minutes. Remove the chicken from the skillet.

3. Add the red pepper, onion, mushrooms, and garlic to the skillet. Sauté for 5 minutes.

4. Add the chicken back to the skillet. Add the tomatoes, tomato paste, wine, and basil. Cover, lower the heat, and simmer for 25 minutes.

Exchanges
1 Carbohydrate
4 Lean Meat

Calories 302
   Calories from Fat . . 84
Total Fat . . . . 9 g
   Saturated Fat . . . . . . 1 g
Cholesterol . . . . 91 mg
Sodium . . . . 113 mg
Carbohydrate . . . . . . 17 g
   Dietary Fiber . . . . . . 4 g
   Sugars . . . . 9 g
Protein . . . . 37 g

Chicken or Turkey Divan

Preparation time: 8 minutes
Cooking time: 20–25 minutes
Serves: 6   Serving size: 1/6 recipe

Chicken Divan is typically based on high-fat cream soups. This version has a rich flavor, but is much lower in calories, fat, and sodium because it uses fat-free, reduced-sodium chicken broth and just a little flour in the sauce. This dish can be made ahead of time and baked later for a quick meal.

1/4	cup stick margarine
3	Tbsp all-purpose flour
1/8	tsp ground white pepper
1	14 1/2-oz can fat-free, reduced-sodium chicken broth
1/2	cup fat-free (skim) milk
2	Tbsp dry white wine
1	1-lb bag frozen broccoli spears or cuts, thawed
1 1/2	cups cooked, skinless, boneless chicken breast, cubed (18 oz precooked)
2	Tbsp grated Parmesan cheese

1. Preheat the oven to 350°F. Spray an 8 × 8-inch square pan with nonstick cooking spray.

2. In a medium skillet, melt the margarine. Add the flour and pepper and stir until smooth. Cook, stirring as needed, until thickened, about 1 minute. Add the broth and cook, stirring constantly, until the mixture thickens and bubbles, 3–4 minutes. Add the milk and wine; reduce the heat to low.

3. Spread the broccoli evenly in the baking pan. Scatter the chicken over the broccoli, then cover evenly with the sauce. Top evenly with the cheese. Bake until lightly browned, 20–25 minutes.

Exchanges
1/2 Carbohydrate
4 Lean Meat

Calories 269
  Calories from Fat . 105
Total Fat . . . . 12 g
  Saturated Fat . . . . . . 3 g
Cholesterol . . . . 75 mg
Sodium . . . . 360 mg
Carbohydrate . . . . . . 8 g
  Dietary Fiber . . . . . . 2 g
  Sugars . . . . 3 g
Protein . . . . 32 g

This dish is great for leftover chicken or turkey—just pick the meat off the bone, measure 1 1/2 cups, place it in a container, and you're ready to go. Serve this dish with rice, pasta, or potatoes. Add a colorful vegetable or fruit, such as sliced carrots or thin slices of cantaloupe.

Chicken Parmesan

Preparation time: 5 minutes
Cooking time: 30 minutes
Serves: 8   Serving size: 1/8 recipe

This recipe, with its vibrant colors, is a cheerful, easy meal! If you like, make your own tomato sauce or add your own spices to a prepared sauce. If you need to watch the sodium in your meal plan, choose a low-sodium brand of prepared sauce, but add 1 Tbsp of oregano or Italian seasonings to spice it up. You can also replace the chicken in this dish with veal or turkey breast.

> 1   26-oz jar seasoned tomato sauce
> 20   oz skinless, boneless chicken breasts
> 1/2   cup shredded part-skim mozzarella cheese
> 1/2   cup grated Parmesan cheese

1. Preheat the oven to 350°F.

2. In a 9 × 13-inch baking pan or large casserole dish, spread half of the tomato sauce. Place the chicken on the sauce, then pour the rest of the sauce over the chicken. Sprinkle the mozzarella cheese on the chicken, then sprinkle on the Parmesan cheese.

3. Cover and bake until bubbly and cheese is lightly browned, 30 minutes.

Exchanges
3 Very Lean Meat
1 Vegetable
1/2 Fat

Calories 153
  Calories from Fat . . 41
Total Fat . . . . 5 g
  Saturated Fat . . . . . . 2 g
Cholesterol . . . . 51 mg
Sodium . . . . 762 mg
Carbohydrate . . . . 7 g
  Dietary Fiber . . . . . . 1 g
  Sugars . . . . 5 g
Protein . . . . 22 g

Serve this dish with bow-tie pasta or another favorite. Start boiling the pasta water about 15 minutes after the chicken goes in the oven. Prepare a fresh salad or heat vegetables right before the chicken is done.

Chicken Paprikash

Preparation time: 20 minutes
Cooking time: 60 minutes
Serves: 7   Serving size: 1/7 recipe

This homey, hearty dish is traditionally served with noodles, spaetzle, or boiled potatoes—but we've saved some carbohydrates by serving it on a bed of green beans. Good-quality paprika is essential to the vivid color and piquant flavor of the paprikash. Look for sweet Hungarian paprika at gourmet grocery stores or better supermarkets, and keep it in the refrigerator to preserve freshness.

> 2 tsp canola oil
> 1 3 1/2-lb chicken, skinned and cut into 7 pieces
> 2 medium onions, thinly sliced
> 1 green bell pepper, chopped
> 3 Tbsp sweet Hungarian paprika
> 2 cups reduced-sodium chicken broth
> 2 cloves garlic, minced
> 1 bay leaf
> 2 10-oz packages French-style frozen green beans
> 3/4 cup fat-free sour cream
> 2 Tbsp fresh lemon juice
> Fresh ground black pepper to taste
> 1/4 cup chopped fresh parsley, for garnish

1. In a large nonstick saucepan, heat the oil. Add half the chicken and cook until golden on both sides, about 10 minutes; transfer to a plate and repeat with the remaining chicken. Drain off all but 1 Tbsp of liquid in the pan.

2. Add the onions and bell pepper and cook, stirring as needed, until slightly browned, about 10 minutes. Sprinkle with the paprika and cook, stirring constantly, until cooked through, about 1 minute. Add the broth, garlic, and bay leaf; bring to a boil.

3. Return the chicken and its accumulated juices to the pan, reduce the heat, and simmer, partially covered, until the chicken is tender and its juices are translucent when pierced with a fork, about 25 minutes. Transfer the chicken to another clean plate.

4. Meanwhile, in a medium saucepan, bring 1 inch water to boiling; add the green beans and cook until just tender, about 2 minutes. Drain and keep warm.

5. Return the sauce to the heat and boil, stirring frequently, until thickened, about 10 minutes. Gently stir in the sour cream, lemon juice, and pepper;

add the chicken and cook until heated through, about 2 minutes.

6. Arrange the green beans on a deep serving platter or bowl; top with the chicken mixture and sprinkle with the parsley.

Exchanges

1/2 Carbohydrate
3 Very Lean Meat
2 Vegetable
1/2 Fat

Calories	232
Calories from Fat	67
Total Fat	7 g
Saturated Fat	2 g
Cholesterol	66 mg
Sodium	242 mg
Carbohydrate	17 g
Dietary Fiber	4 g
Sugars	8 g
Protein	25 g

Chicken Pot Pie

Preparation time: 25 minutes (excluding crust)
Cooking time: 1 hour
Serves: 8   Serving size: 1/8 recipe

Pot pies are pastry-covered dishes made with meat and vegetables in a gravy sauce. Most likely they got their start in the days when no food was wasted and all leftovers found their way into the next meal.

3 medium potatoes, peeled and cubed
3 large carrots, peeled and sliced
2 celery stalks, sliced
1 medium onion, chopped
1/4 tsp salt
1 cup fresh or frozen green beans or frozen mixed vegetables
4 Tbsp stick margarine
4 Tbsp all-purpose flour
1 14 1/2-oz can fat-free, low-sodium chicken broth
1 cup low-fat (1%) milk
1/2 tsp dried rosemary
1/4 tsp ground white pepper
2 cups cubed, cooked, skinless chicken breast
1 recipe Buttery Pie Crust (p. 185), rolled to a 9 × 13-inch rectangle

Exchanges
2 Starch
1 Lean Meat
1 Vegetable
2 1/2 Fat

Calories 350
  Calories from Fat . 145
Total Fat . . . . 16 g
  Saturated Fat . . . . . . 3 g
Cholesterol . . . . 35 mg
Sodium . . . . 327 mg
Carbohydrate . . . . . . 34 g
  Dietary Fiber . . . . . . 3 g
  Sugars . . . . 6 g
Protein . . . . 17 g

1. Preheat the oven to 375°F. Spray a 9 × 13-inch pan with nonstick cooking spray.

2. In a large pot, add the potatoes, carrots, celery, onion, and salt and enough water to cover the potatoes by 1 inch; boil 5 minutes. Add the beans and continue cooking for another 2 minutes; if using frozen beans or vegetables, add during the last two minutes of cooking time. Reserve 1/2 cup of the cooking water; set aside. Drain and keep warm.

3. In a large skillet, melt the margarine. Stir in the flour until blended; then add the chicken broth. Cook, stirring constantly, until thickened, 3–4 minutes. Stir in the reserved cooking water, milk, rosemary, and pepper.

4. Sprinkle the vegetables and chicken in the bottom of the prepared pan, then pour on the gravy. Top with the prepared pie crust, pressing to form a rim. Cut four half-inch slits in the top of the crust. Bake until browned, about 1 hour. Let stand 5 minutes before cutting.

Chile Con Queso

Preparation time: 10 minutes
Cooking time: 12 minutes
Serves: 6   Serving size: 1 cup

Chile Con Queso means "chile with cheese." This vegetarian chile is made with black beans and ancho chile powder so it has a real zip! Ancho chile powder is found right with the other spices in your grocery store, or you can try mail order spice companies on the net. It has a rich flavor—get it while it's hot!

1   28-oz can low-sodium whole tomatoes in juice
2   cloves garlic, minced
1   medium onion, finely chopped
3/4 tsp ground ancho chile powder
3/4 tsp chile powder
1/4 tsp ground cumin
1   15-oz can black beans with juice
1   4-oz can chopped green chiles
3   Tbsp minced fresh parsley
1   Tbsp red wine vinegar
1/2 cup shredded Monterey Jack cheese
2   Tbsp minced cilantro

Exchanges
1 Starch
2 Vegetable
1/2 Fat

Calories 144
   Calories from Fat . . 31
Total Fat . . . . 3 g
   Saturated Fat . . . . . . 2 g
Cholesterol . . . . 8 mg
Sodium . . . . 441 mg
Carbohydrate . . . . . . 21 g
   Dietary Fiber . . . . . . 7 g
   Sugars . . . . 7 g
Protein . . . . 8 g

1. In a large nonstick skillet, over medium-high heat, cook the tomatoes, garlic, onion, ancho chile powder, chile powder, and cumin, stirring occasionally, until mixture starts to thicken, 8–10 minutes. Turn the heat to low and add the beans, chiles, 2 Tbsp of the parsley, and the vinegar; cook, stirring occasionally, until bubbly, about 5 minutes. Stir in the cheese.

2. Place in a serving dish or in individual bowls; top with the cilantro and remaining parsley.

Instead of stirring the cheese into the chile, you can sprinkle it on top of each serving. Either way, top each serving with some minced fresh parsley. This chile is quite thick, so it makes a great dip. Serve it with cut-up red and green bell peppers or cucumber slices for dipping.

Chicken and Rice Casserole

Preparation time: 45 minutes
Cooking time: 25 minutes
Serves: 7   Serving size: 1/7 recipe

If you're nostalgic for Mom's casserole—the one she made with 2 cans of condensed soup—you'll love this fresher, lighter version.

- 2 tsp canola oil
- 1 3 1/2-lb chicken, cut up and skinned
- 1 medium onion, finely chopped
- 4 stalks celery, finely chopped
- 1 cup sliced fresh mushrooms
- 1 medium zucchini, diced
- 3 cups cooked brown or white rice
- 1/2 cup low-sodium chicken broth
- 1/2 cup fat-free sour cream
- 2 tsp fresh thyme or 1 tsp dried
- 1/2 tsp ground black pepper
- 1/4 tsp ground allspice
- 1 Tbsp plain dried bread crumbs
- 1/4 tsp paprika

1. In a large nonstick skillet, heat 1 tsp of the oil. Cook chicken in two batches until it is lightly browned on both sides, about 10 minutes. Transfer the chicken to a plate; keep warm. Remove all but 1 tsp of the liquid from the skillet.

2. Preheat the oven to 350°F. Spray a 9 × 13-inch baking pan with nonstick cooking spray.

3. Return the skillet to the heat and cook the onion and celery, stirring as needed, until the onion is translucent, about 8 minutes. Add the mushrooms and zucchini; continue cooking until the mushrooms release and reabsorb their juices, about 5 minutes.

4. Stir in the rice, broth, sour cream, thyme, pepper, and allspice; spread the mixture evenly in the bottom of the prepared baking pan. Top with the chicken in a single layer. Cover with foil and bake 15 minutes.

Exchanges
1 1/2 Starch
2 Very Lean Meat
1 Vegetable
12 Fat

Calories 287
  Calories from Fat . . 71
Total Fat . . . . 8 g
  Saturated Fat . . . . . . 2 g
Cholesterol . . . . 66 mg
Sodium . . . . 150 mg
Carbohydrate . . . . . . 28 g
  Dietary Fiber . . . . . . 3 g
  Sugars . . . . 4 g
Protein . . . . 26 g

5. Meanwhile, in a small bowl with a fork, stir together the bread crumbs, the remaining tsp oil, and the paprika.

6. Uncover the chicken and sprinkle evenly with the bread crumb mixture. Return to the oven and bake, uncovered, until the chicken is cooked through and the juices run clear, about 25 minutes.

Eggplant Parmigiana

Preparation time: 45 minutes
Cooking time: 1 hour
Serves: 8   Serving size: 1/8 recipe

Eggplant seems to soak up its weight in oil when it's fried, so simply baking the slices instead cuts the fat dramatically. To compensate, we brightened up the tomato sauce—you'll taste fresh tomato, not fat. The secret: using canned tomatoes in juice, not puree, so the clean tomato flavor shines through. If you don't like chunks of tomato in your Parmigiana, you can puree the tomatoes in a food processor or blender first, or use an immersion blender to prepare a smooth sauce right in the pot.

> 2 tsp olive oil, preferably extra-virgin
> 3 eggs
> 3 Tbsp water
> 1 1/2 cups plain dried bread crumbs
> 1/2 cup grated Parmesan cheese
> 1 Tbsp Italian seasoning
> 2 eggplants, peeled and sliced 1/4 inch thick (about 2 lb)
> 3 15-oz cans diced tomatoes in juice
> 2 cloves garlic, minced
> 1 cup shredded part-skim mozzarella cheese

1. Preheat the oven to 400°F. Lightly coat 2 baking sheets with 1 tsp oil each. Spray a 9 × 13-inch baking pan with nonstick cooking spray.

2. In a shallow bowl, beat the eggs with the water. In another shallow bowl, combine the bread crumbs, 1/4 cup of the Parmesan cheese, and the Italian seasoning.

3. Dip the eggplant slices into the egg mixture, then coat with the bread crumb mixture. Discard any leftover egg or bread crumb mixture. Arrange the slices, one layer deep, on the prepared baking sheets. Bake until lightly browned, about 15 minutes, then turn the slices and bake until crisp-edged, 15–20 minutes more.

Exchanges

1 Starch
1 Lean Meat
2 Vegetable
1 Fat

Calories 219
  Calories from Fat . . 74
Total Fat . . . . 8 g
  Saturated Fat . . . . . . 4 g
Cholesterol . . . . 84 mg
Sodium . . . . 666 mg
Carbohydrate . . . . . . 26 g
  Dietary Fiber . . . . . . 4 g
  Sugars . . . . 10 g
Protein . . . . 13 g

4. In a medium saucepan, combine the tomatoes with the garlic. Bring to a boil, covered, stirring as needed; lower the heat and simmer 15 minutes. Set aside.

5. Spread about 1/2 cup of the sauce in the bottom of the prepared baking dish. Arrange a single layer of eggplant slices over the sauce, then top with another layer of sauce. Sprinkle with 1/3 of the mozzarella cheese, then top with another layer of eggplant slices. Repeat to make 2 more layers, then sprinkle with the remaining 1/4 cup Parmesan cheese. Bake until bubbly, about 20 minutes.

Creamy Mashed Potatoes

Preparation time: 10 minutes
Cooking time: 15 minutes
Serves: 6   Serving size: 1 cup

Potatoes and sour cream are a favorite combination. With this recipe, butter-milk, not sour cream, provides the creamy and tangy flavor. Despite butter-milk *sounding* high in fat, it actually is low in fat and a great partner for potatoes.

    6 medium russet potatoes, peeled and cut into 2-inch
       pieces
    3 Tbsp stick margarine
  1/2 cup low-fat (1%) buttermilk

1. In a large saucepan, simmer the potatoes in enough water to cover until tender, about 15 minutes. Drain well.

2. Add the margarine to the hot potatoes. When melted, 30–60 seconds, mash the potatoes with a potato masher or with an electric mixer until fluffy, 2–3 minutes. Pour the buttermilk on the potatoes and continue mashing until texture is smooth, 2 minutes. Serve immediately.

Exchanges
1 1/2 Starch
1 Fat

Calories 157
    Calories from Fat . . 54
Total Fat . . . . 6 g
    Saturated Fat . . . . . . 1 g
Cholesterol . . . . 1 mg
Sodium . . . . 93 mg
Carbohydrate . . . . . . 24 g
    Dietary Fiber . . . . . . 2 g
    Sugars . . . . 3 g
Protein . . . . 3 g

Enchilada Casserole

Preparation time: 15 minutes
Cooking time: 25 minutes
Serves: 6   Serving size: 1 enchilada

This easy dish is full of flavor with its green chilis, fresh cilantro, garlic, and red peppers! And, if you're not a cilantro fan, the dish is still wonderfully spicy without it. The low-fat Monterey Jack cheese saves you unwanted calories and fat. For added pizzazz, top with a dollop of fat-free sour cream.

6 corn tortillas
1 tsp olive oil
1/2 medium onion, chopped
1 small red bell pepper, chopped
1 clove garlic, minced
1 cup canned kidney beans with juice, coarsely mashed
1 14-oz can low-sodium whole tomatoes in juice, drained and chopped
1 4-oz can green chiles and juice
1 Tbsp minced cilantro (optional)
1 Tbsp fresh lime juice
1/4 tsp ground cumin
1 cup shredded low-fat Monterey Jack cheese

1. Preheat the oven to 350°F. Spray an 8 × 8-inch pan with nonstick cooking spray. Warm the tortillas according to package directions.

2. In a medium nonstick skillet, heat the oil. Add the onion, bell pepper, and garlic; cook, stirring as needed, until the onion is translucent, about 5 minutes.

3. In a medium bowl, combine the beans, tomatoes, chiles, cilantro, lime juice, and cumin. Add the onion mixture and stir until blended.

4. Cover the bottom of the pan with 3 tortillas; add half of the bean mixture, top with half of the cheese; layer with the remaining 3 tortillas, beans, and cheese. Bake covered until bubbly for 20 minutes. Remove cover and continue baking until cheese melts, about 5 minutes. Serve immediately.

Exchanges

1 Starch
1 Vegetable
1 Fat

Calories 152
  Calories from Fat . . 32
Total Fat . . . . 4 g
  Saturated Fat . . . . . . 2 g
Cholesterol . . . . 7 mg
Sodium . . . . 363 mg
Carbohydrate . . . . . . 24 g
  Dietary Fiber . . . . . . 5 g
  Sugars . . . . 4 g
Protein . . . . 8 g

Green Bean Casserole

Preparation time: 15 minutes
Cooking time: 30 minutes
Serves: 6   Serving size: 1/2 cup

Right out of the '50s, this casserole was designed to be easy, not healthy, with canned cream soup and greasy fried onion bits among its ingredients. Our lighter, fresher version takes a little longer to make, but is well worth the trouble!

2	tsp canola oil
1	large onion, thinly sliced
1	medium onion, finely chopped
3 1/4	cups sliced mushrooms
1	clove garlic, minced
1/4	cup all-purpose flour
1	16-oz can low-fat, low-sodium chicken broth
1	bay leaf
1/2	tsp dried thyme
	Pinch freshly ground nutmeg
3/4	cup low-fat sour cream
	Fresh ground black pepper to taste
1/2	cup cornflake crumbs
1	lb frozen green beans, or 4 cups lightly steamed green beans

1. In a large nonstick skillet, heat 1 tsp oil over low heat. Add the sliced onion and cook, stirring occasionally, until soft and golden brown, about 20 minutes. Set aside. (This step may be done up to 2 days in advance; store, covered, in the refrigerator.)

2. Preheat the oven to 425°F.

3. In a large nonstick saucepan or Dutch oven, heat the remaining oil over medium heat. Add the chopped onion and cook, stirring frequently, until translucent, about 4–5 minutes. Stir in the mushrooms and garlic; continue cooking until the mushrooms release their juices, about 4 minutes.

4. Sprinkle the flour over the mushrooms. Cook, stirring, 2–3 minutes, then gradually stir in the broth. Add the bay leaf, thyme, and nutmeg; simmer, stirring occasionally, until slightly thickened, about 5 minutes. Remove from heat; stir in the sour cream, season with pepper, and remove the bay leaf. Set aside.

5. In a small bowl, combine the reserved onion topping with the cornflake crumbs, coating thoroughly.

6. In a 2-qt baking dish, add green beans. Top with the sauce, then evenly scatter the onion mixture on top. Bake until bubbling, 20–25 minutes.

Exchanges

1 Starch
2 Vegetable
1/2 Fat

Calories 155
  Calories from Fat . . 41
Total Fat . . . . 5 g
  Saturated Fat . . . . . . 1 g
Cholesterol . . . . 10 mg
Sodium . . . . 268 mg
Carbohydrate . . . . . . 25 g
  Dietary Fiber . . . . . . 4 g
  Sugars . . . . 9 g
Protein . . . . 7 g

Macaroni and Cheese

Preparation time: 20 minutes
Cooking time: 30 minutes
Serves: 6   Serving size: 1 cup

Three different cheeses lend their power to this dish: sharp cheddar, for body and taste; processed cheese, for creamy texture; and Parmesan, to intensify the other cheese flavors. Adding artichoke hearts is a great way to sneak in some extra vegetables, but you can leave them out if you like. The technique of stirring the macaroni as it bakes, while adding more cheese and milk, helps make the cheese sauce wonderfully creamy. It's worth the effort.

9 oz elbow macaroni
1 10-oz pkg frozen artichoke hearts
1 cup shredded extra-sharp cheddar cheese
1/4 cup shredded processed cheese, such as American
2 Tbsp grated Parmesan cheese
1 12-oz can evaporated fat-free milk, divided
2 eggs
2 tsp dry mustard, dissolved in 1 Tbsp water
1/2 tsp ground black pepper
Pinch cayenne pepper

Exchanges

3 Starch
2 Lean Meat

Calories	352
Calories from Fat	97
Total Fat	11 g
Saturated Fat	6 g
Cholesterol	97 mg
Sodium	342 mg
Carbohydrate	43 g
Dietary Fiber	3 g
Sugars	8 g
Protein	20 g

1. Cook the macaroni according to package directions, adding the artichoke hearts 3 minutes before the pasta is finished cooking. When the artichokes are cooked through and the pasta is nearly tender, drain and keep warm.

2. Preheat the oven to 350°F. Spray a 2-qt baking dish with nonstick cooking spray. In a small bowl, combine the cheddar, American, and Parmesan cheeses; set aside.

3. In a medium saucepan over low heat, whisk together 1 cup of the evaporated milk, the eggs, the mustard mixture, and the black and cayenne pepper; heat, whisking constantly, just until warmed through, about 2 minutes. Remove from the heat and stir in the cooked macaroni mixture, and half of the cheese mixture. Pour into the prepared pan and bake 5 minutes.

4. Stir the macaroni and return it to the oven 5 more minutes, then stir in half of the remaining evaporated milk and cheeses. Return it to the oven 10 more minutes, then stir in the remaining evaporated milk and cheeses. Bake until lightly browned along the edges, 10 minutes more. Serve immediately.

Meatloaf

Preparation time: 10 minutes
Cooking time: 90 minutes
Serves: 10   Serving size: 1 slice

This meatloaf is made with ground turkey breast and lean ground beef so it's low in fat but packed with flavor. Eat it hot or enjoy it in a sandwich the next day.

1	lb ground skinless turkey breast
1	lb lean ground beef
1/2	medium onion, minced
1	clove garlic, minced
3	Tbsp minced fresh parsley
1	egg
1/4	cup low-fat (1%) milk
1	tsp dry mustard
1/4	tsp salt
1/4	tsp ground white pepper
1/8	tsp nutmeg
2	slices white bread, lightly toasted and made into coarse crumbs
2	Tbsp ketchup
2	Tbsp water

1. Preheat the oven to 350°F.

2. In a large bowl, combine the meats with your hands or a large fork. Blend in the onion, garlic, and parsley; set aside.

3. In a medium bowl, whisk the egg until frothy, about 1 minute. Add the milk, mustard, salt, pepper, and nutmeg and whisk to blend. Add the bread crumbs and let stand for 5 minutes.

4. Add the egg mixture to the meat mixture and blend well, about 1 minute. Spread evenly into a 9 × 5-inch loaf pan.

5. In a small bowl, combine the ketchup and water until blended. Spread on top of the meat. Bake until the meat is no longer pink, about 90 minutes.

Exchanges

1/2 Starch
3 Very Lean Meat

Calories	139
Calories from Fat	30
Total Fat	3 g
Saturated Fat	1 g
Cholesterol	74 mg
Sodium	185 mg
Carbohydrate	4 g
Dietary Fiber	0 g
Sugars	1 g
Protein	21 g

Serve this meatloaf with our Creamy Mashed Potatoes, p. 96. Add a fresh salad or other vegetables, such as green beans or broccoli spears.

Quick Beef Stroganoff

Preparation time: 15 minutes
Cooking time: 15 minutes
Serves: 8   Serving size: 1 1/2 cups

A delectable sauce makes this an easy, great meal. Serve with a generous serving of cut green beans or broccoli spears.

- 12 oz egg noodles
- 1 Tbsp olive oil
- 1 medium onion, chopped
- 1 lb top round steak, trimmed and sliced 1/4 inch thick
- 1/2 tsp garlic powder
- 1/8 tsp ground black pepper
- 1 10 3/4-oz can low-fat, low-sodium cream of mushroom soup
- 1 1/4 cups low-fat (1%) milk
- 1 Tbsp all-purpose flour
- 1/2 cup reduced-fat sour cream

1. Cook the noodles according to package directions, omitting the salt. Drain and place in a large casserole dish; keep warm.

2. In a large saucepan, heat the oil. Cook the onion, stirring occasionally, until it starts to turn opaque, about 3 minutes. Reduce the heat to low; add the meat and cook, stirring as needed, until the meat is no longer pink, about 5 minutes. Stir in the garlic powder and pepper.

3. Add the soup, stir in, then fill the empty soup can with cold milk. Combine half of the milk with the meat mixture and stir. Add the flour to the remaining milk in the can and stir until smooth. Pour into the meat mixture and stir until smooth. Cook about 5 minutes. Stir in the sour cream and continue to cook until sauce is again heated through, 2 minutes.

4. Pour the meat and sauce onto the noodles in the casserole dish; serve immediately.

Exchanges
2 1/2 Starch
2 Lean Meat

Calories 308
  Calories from Fat . . 75
Total Fat . . . . 8 g
  Saturated Fat . . . . . . 3 g
Cholesterol . . . . 77 mg
Sodium . . . . 198 mg
Carbohydrate . . . . . . 39 g
  Dietary Fiber . . . . . . 2 g
  Sugars . . . . 5 g
Protein . . . . 19 g

Scalloped Potatoes

Preparation time: 20 minutes
Cooking time: 1 hour
Serves: 8   Serving size: 1/8 recipe

The butter and whole milk have been replaced with margarine and low-fat milk in this traditional favorite. The addition of fresh dill and rutabaga perk up the dish and make it possible to use less cheese without losing flavor. Don't say no to the rutabaga until you've tried it! Or, try celery root (the base of a celery stalk) instead of the rutabaga.

    5 medium potatoes, peeled
    2 Tbsp stick margarine
    2 Tbsp all-purpose flour
    2 cups low-fat (1%) milk
  1/4 small rutabaga, peeled and shredded (about 1/2 cup)
  1/2 medium onion, chopped
    1 Tbsp fresh dill, minced
  1/2 tsp salt
  1/2 tsp dry mustard
  1/4 tsp ground white pepper
  1/2 cup shredded cheddar cheese

1. Preheat the oven to 350°F. Spray a 9 × 13-inch pan with nonstick cooking spray.

2. Fill a medium bowl with cold water. Slice the potatoes 1/16 inch thick, dropping them directly into the water as you work to prevent browning. Set aside.

3. In a large nonstick skillet, melt the margarine. Add the flour and stir over medium heat until blended, about 1 minute. Add the milk and cook, stirring constantly, until the mixture thickens and bubbles, about 3–4 minutes. Stir in the rutabaga, onion, dill, salt, mustard, and pepper and heat 1 minute more. Remove from the heat.

4. Drain the potatoes and place in the prepared pan. Pour the sauce over the potatoes to coat. Sprinkle with the cheese.

5. Bake, uncovered, until browned, about 1 hour.

Exchanges
1 1/2 Starch
1 Fat

Calories 155
  Calories from Fat . . 54
Total Fat . . . . 6 g
  Saturated Fat . . . . . . 3 g
Cholesterol . . . . 10 mg
Sodium . . . . 260 mg
Carbohydrate . . . . . . 20 g
  Dietary Fiber . . . . . . 2 g
  Sugars . . . . 5 g
Protein . . . . 6 g

The air oxidizes peeled potatoes and apples and turns them brown. Placing potatoes in water, as we do here, or adding lemon juice to sliced apples is one way of preventing unsightly oxidation!

Shepherd's Pie

Preparation time: 25 minutes
Cooking time: 40 minutes
Serves: 8   Serving size: 1 cup

In England and Ireland, Shepherd's Pie was made with lamb. It might be better to call this recipe Farmer's Pie, since it's made with lean ground turkey breast instead of lamb. This pie is packed with vegetables, making it a complete meal, and is very easy to prepare. You'll have great leftovers the next day.

4	medium potatoes, peeled and cubed
1	lb ground skinless turkey breast
2	carrots, thinly sliced
1	medium onion, chopped
1	red bell pepper, chopped
1	celery stalk, chopped
2	cloves garlic, minced
1	10 3/4-oz can low-fat, low-sodium cream of chicken soup
1/2	cup low-fat (1%) milk
1	cup frozen corn
1	cup fat-free sour cream
2	Tbsp minced fresh parsley

1. Preheat the oven to 350°F. Spray a 9 × 13-inch pan with nonstick cooking spray.

2. In a medium saucepan, add the potatoes and enough water to cover by 1 inch. Cook over medium heat until tender, about 20 minutes.

3. Meanwhile, in a large nonstick skillet, cook the turkey until browned, about 5–7 minutes. Add the carrots, onion, pepper, celery, and garlic and cook until the vegetables are tender but firm, about 10 minutes. Blend in the soup, milk, and corn.

4. Add the sour cream to the drained potatoes; mash until fluffy.

5. Spread the meat and vegetable mixture in the prepared pan. Spread the potatoes evenly on top.

Exchanges
1 1/2 Starch
2 Very Lean Meat
1 Vegetable

Calories 204
  Calories from Fat . . 14
Total Fat . . . . 2 g
  Saturated Fat . . . . . . 1 g
Cholesterol . . . . 38 mg
Sodium . . . . 233 mg
Carbohydrate . . . . . . 31 g
  Dietary Fiber . . . . . . 3 g
  Sugars . . . . 8 g
Protein . . . . 17 g

6. Bake, uncovered, until heated through and the potatoes are browned, about 40 minutes. (For crustier potatoes, place under the broiler for 1–2 minutes after baking.) Sprinkle with parsley.

If you do not have a non-stick skillet, use a regular one and spray it with non-stick cooking spray. This may result in some of the turkey sticking to the bottom of the pan. Don't despair! This wonderful browning can enhance the flavor of the pie. After cooking the turkey, add 1 Tbsp of water to the skillet and scrape the bottom. Add the browned mixture to the rest of the meat and vegetables. You'll be amazed at how easily the browning (essence) comes off the pan; easier than scrubbing later, and the flavor becomes part of the dish.

Shrimp Etouffée

Preparation time: 1 hour
Cooking time: 30 minutes
Serves: 4   Serving size: 1 1/2 cups

In this complex Louisiana specialty, shrimp (or, if you can get them, crayfish) are smothered (etouffée) in a mixture of simmered aromatic vegetables. Thanks to Fat-Free Brown Roux (see recipe, p. 49), we've trimmed the fat considerably. It requires some time, but each step is critical in adding a layer of flavor, including simmering the shrimp in their flavorful shells. You can't take any short-cuts on this dish! Serve it with hot cooked rice and a crisp green salad on the side.

Bouillon
- 3 cups water
- 1 medium onion, quartered
- 2 cloves garlic, flattened with a knife
- 1 tsp fresh ground black pepper
- 1/2 tsp dried thyme
- 1/2 tsp coriander seeds
- 1/2 tsp dried red pepper flakes
- 1 bay leaf
- 1 1/2 lb large shrimp, shells on

Etouffée
- 1 Tbsp canola oil
- 1 medium onion, chopped
- 1 green or red bell pepper, chopped
- 2 stalks celery, chopped
- 4 green onions, chopped
- 1 jalapeño pepper, finely chopped
- 2 large cloves garlic, minced
- 2 Tbsp Brown Roux (see recipe, p. 49)
- Fresh lemon juice to taste
- Cayenne pepper to taste
- Fresh ground pepper to taste

Exchanges
1 Carbohydrate
3 Very Lean Meat
1/2 Fat

Calories 204
  Calories from Fat . . 45
Total Fat . . . . 5 g
  Saturated Fat . . . . . . 0 g
Cholesterol . . . . 218 mg
Sodium . . . . 274 mg
Carbohydrate . . . . . . 14 g
  Dietary Fiber . . . . . . 3 g
  Sugars . . . . 6 g
Protein . . . . 26 g

1. To prepare the bouillon, in a large saucepan, combine the water, onion, garlic, black pepper, thyme, coriander, pepper flakes, and bay leaf; bring to a boil. Add the shrimp; reduce the heat, cover, and simmer 1 minute. Remove from the heat and let stand 10 minutes.

2. With a slotted spoon, transfer the shrimp to a bowl; when cool enough to handle, peel the shrimp and set aside. Discard the shells. Strain the broth and return it to the saucepan. Bring to a boil and cook, uncovered, until the liquid is reduced to 1 1/2 cups, about 10 minutes. Set aside.

3. Meanwhile, in a large, nonstick saucepan, heat the oil. Add the onion, bell pepper, celery, green onions, jalapeño pepper, and garlic; cook, stirring as needed, until the vegetables are soft, about 10 minutes. Sprinkle with the roux and stir to incorporate. Add the reserved bouillon and simmer until heated through, about 2 minutes. Season with lemon juice, cayenne, and ground pepper to taste. Pour the sauce over the shrimp.

Spanakopita (Greek Spinach Pie)

Preparation time: 25 minutes
Cooking time: 40 minutes
Serves: 12   Serving size: 1/12 recipe

Packed with spinach, Spanakopita is a great way to eat your vegetables—were it not for the rich feta cheese and butter-doused layers of phyllo pastry. We've cut the fat (and the feta) and boosted flavor with dill, parsley, and lemon zest. And, instead of butter between the pastry layers, a thin layer of butter-oil blend and some bread crumbs does the trick.

- 1 tsp olive oil
- 1 bunch green onions, white and green parts, chopped (about 1 cup)
- 2 lb fresh spinach, washed, steamed, and chopped (or 3 10-oz pkg frozen chopped spinach, thawed)
- 2 eggs, beaten
- 4 oz crumbled feta cheese
- 1/2 cup low-fat (1%) cottage cheese
- 1 cup chopped fresh parsley
- 1/2 cup chopped fresh dill
- 1 Tbsp grated lemon zest
- 2 Tbsp unsalted butter
- 2 Tbsp canola oil
- 8 sheets phyllo dough, thawed if frozen
- 3 Tbsp plain dried bread crumbs

1. In a large skillet, heat the oil. Add the green onions and cook, stirring as needed, until softened, about 8 minutes. Let cool slightly.

2. In a large bowl, combine the spinach, eggs, feta, cottage cheese, parsley, dill, and zest; stir in the cooled onions.

3. Preheat the oven to 375°F. Spray a 9 × 13-inch baking dish with nonstick cooking spray.

4. In a small microwave-safe bowl, melt the butter; stir in the oil and set aside.

5. Lay the phyllo dough on a work surface; cover with plastic wrap, then a damp towel. Carefully remove 1 sheet, immediately replacing the cover on the remaining phyllo,

Exchanges
1 Starch
1 1/2 Fat

Calories 157
  Calories from Fat . . 73
Total Fat . . . . 8 g
  Saturated Fat . . . . . . 3 g
Cholesterol . . . . 49 mg
Sodium . . . . 287 mg
Carbohydrate . . . . . . 15 g
  Dietary Fiber . . . . . . 2 g
  Sugars . . . . 2 g
Protein . . . . 7 g

and place in and up the sides of the prepared pan. Brush lightly with the butter mixture and sprinkle with a thin layer of bread crumbs. Repeat with 3 more phyllo sheets, then spread the spinach mixture over the layered phyllo. Top with 4 more sheets, brushing each one with the oil mixture and sprinkling all but the top layer with the crumbs.

6. Roll the overhanging phyllo from the sides to form a border all along the pie. Carefully cut the pie into 12 pieces, cutting nearly through to the bottom (don't cut all the way through, or the filling will leak out into the pan). Bake until lightly browned and crisp, about 40 minutes. Let stand a few minutes, then cut completely.

Swedish Meatballs

Preparation time: 50 minutes (includes 30 minutes chilling time)
Cooking time: 60 minutes
Serves: 12   Serving size: 4 meatballs

These Swedish meatballs are made with ground turkey breast and lean pork instead of the traditional pork-beef-veal combination. We've also eliminated the fatty gravy. They can be made at least 24 hours ahead and stored in a covered container. Serve them as an entrée, in pasta sauce, or as meatball sandwiches.

1	egg
1/2	cup low-fat (1%) milk
2	slices white bread, lightly toasted and made into coarse crumbs
1/2	small onion, minced
2	Tbsp minced fresh parsley
1/2	tsp salt (optional)
1/4	tsp ground allspice
1/4	tsp nutmeg
1	lb ground skinless turkey breast
1/2	lb lean ground pork
3	Tbsp all-purpose flour
2	tsp vegetable oil

Exchanges

1/2 Starch
2 Very Lean Meat

Calories 106
  Calories from Fat . . 24
Total Fat . . . . 3 g
  Saturated Fat . . . . . . 1 g
Cholesterol . . . . 54 mg
Sodium . . . . 65 mg
Carbohydrate . . . . 5 g
  Dietary Fiber . . . . . . 0 g
  Sugars . . . . 1 g
Protein . . . . 15 g

1. In a large bowl, whisk the egg with the milk and bread crumbs; let stand for 5 minutes. Add the onion, parsley, salt, allspice, and nutmeg; blend well. Add the meats and stir with a fork until well blended. Cover and chill for at least 30 minutes.

2. Sprinkle the flour on a piece of waxed paper and place next to the meat bowl. Shape the meat into 48 meatballs, about 1 Tbsp each. Dip each meatball lightly in the flour and place on a baking sheet. Set aside.

3. In a large nonstick skillet, heat 1 tsp of the oil. Add half the meatballs and cook until browned all over, 5 minutes. Cover and cook the meatballs until the meat is no longer pink, 20–25 minutes, turning occasionally. (Remaining meatballs should be refrigerated.) Transfer the cooked meatballs to a bowl, cover, and keep warm.

4. Remove any small meat pieces from the skillet. Repeat step 3 with the remaining meatballs.

Tuna Noodle Casserole

Preparation time: 10 minutes
Cooking time: 25 minutes
Serves: 6   Serving size: 1/6 recipe

The savory spices in this recipe have been increased to compensate for the reduced fat and salt from the canned soup. Extra celery gives an appealing crunch.

1/4	cup stick margarine
3	Tbsp all-purpose flour
1/4	tsp ground white pepper
1	14 1/2-oz can fat-free, low-sodium chicken broth
1/2	cup fat-free (skim) milk
2	6 1/2-oz cans water-packed tuna, drained
2	celery stalks, finely chopped
1/4	small onion, minced
1/4	cup minced fresh parsley
1	clove garlic, minced
4	cups cooked wide egg noodles

1. Preheat the oven to 350°F. Spray an 8 × 8-inch pan with nonstick cooking spray.

2. In a medium skillet, melt the margarine. Add the flour and pepper; stir until smooth. Cook until thickened, about 1 minute. Add the broth and stir until the mixture thickens and bubbles, about 3–4 minutes.

3. Reduce the heat to low and add the milk; heat until slightly thickened, 1 minute. Add the tuna, celery, onion, parsley, and garlic; stir until well blended. Gently stir in the noodles. Pour the mixture into the prepared baking pan. Cover and bake for 20 minutes. Uncover and continue baking until bubbly, about 5 minutes.

Exchanges

2 Starch
2 Lean Meat
1/2 Fat

Calories	305
Calories from Fat	87
Total Fat	10 g
Saturated Fat	1 g
Cholesterol	51 mg
Sodium	441 mg
Carbohydrate	32 g
Dietary Fiber	2 g
Sugars	3 g
Protein	21 g

Turkey Tacos

Preparation time: 20 minutes
Cooking time: 20 minutes
Serves: 8   Serving size: 1 taco

You'll never have to buy another package of prepared taco mix to make a taco dinner again! This recipe makes a fast and healthy dinner in about 20 minutes, using lean ground turkey breast and robust spices.

1	tsp ground cumin
1	tsp chili powder
1	tsp dried oregano
1/2	tsp salt
1/8	tsp cayenne pepper
1	8-oz can unsalted tomato sauce
4	Tbsp water, divided
1	lb ground skinless turkey breast
8	6-inch corn or flour tortillas
2	tomatoes, finely chopped
1	cup lettuce or spinach, finely chopped
1/2	cup shredded cheddar cheese
1/2	cup fat-free sour cream

1. In a small bowl, combine the cumin, chili powder, oregano, salt, and cayenne pepper. Stir in the tomato sauce and 2 Tbsp water and stir to blend. Continue heating until hot, about 5 minutes.

2. In a large nonstick skillet, over medium-high heat, cook the turkey until browned, about 10 minutes. Reduce the heat to low and stir in the tomato sauce, the reserved spice mixture, and 2 Tbsp water. Cook, stirring occasionally until bubbling, about 5 minutes.

3. To make the tacos, heat the tortillas according to package directions. Fill each taco with a small amount of the meat mixture, then tomatoes, lettuce, and 1 Tbsp each of the cheese and sour cream. Fold the tortilla in half and serve.

Exchanges

1 Starch
2 Very Lean Meat
1/2 Fat

Calories 171	
Calories from Fat . . 32	
Total Fat . . . . 4 g	
Saturated Fat . . . . . . 2 g	
Cholesterol . . . . 41 mg	
Sodium . . . . 283 mg	
Carbohydrate . . . . . . 19 g	
Dietary Fiber . . . . . . 2 g	
Sugars . . . . 3 g	
Protein . . . . 17 g	

We've used soft tortillas, which are lower in fat than the hard-shell type. If you prefer hard-shell tacos, you can easily use half the shredded cheese amount to even out the fat. To keep soft tortillas from drying out when warmed, heat them in the microwave between sheets of dampened paper towels for 15–20 seconds each.

Pizza & Pasta

Recipes

Baked Ziti with Eggplant

Preparation time: 20 minutes
Cooking time: 25 minutes
Serves: 6   Serving size: 1/6 recipe

There's no meat in this dish, yet no one will miss it: the meaty eggplant and fragrant basil will make mouths water.

1 lb eggplant, peeled and diced
1 clove garlic, minced
4 fresh basil leaves, finely chopped
1/4 cup minced fresh parsley
4 oz ziti
1 15-oz can sodium-free tomato sauce
1/2 cup shredded part-skim mozzarella cheese

1. Preheat the oven to 350°F. Spray an 8 × 8-inch pan with nonstick cooking spray.

2. In a medium saucepan, add the eggplant and enough water to cover. Bring to a boil and cook until tender but not mushy, about 10 minutes; drain. Add the garlic, basil, and parsley; stir to combine. Cover and let stand until the flavors are blended, about 10 minutes.

3. Meanwhile, cook the ziti according to package directions, omitting the salt. Drain and keep warm.

4. Add the tomato sauce to the eggplant mixture and stir lightly until blended.

5. Spread the ziti in the bottom of the prepared baking pan and top with the eggplant mixture. Sprinkle evenly with the cheese. Bake, uncovered, until the cheese melts, about 25 minutes.

Exchanges

1 Starch
1 Vegetable
1/2 Fat

Calories 127
  Calories from Fat . . 17
Total Fat . . . . 2 g
  Saturated Fat . . . . . . 1 g
Cholesterol . . . . 5 mg
Sodium . . . . 65 mg
Carbohydrate . . . . . . 22 g
  Dietary Fiber . . . . . . 2 g
  Sugars . . . . 6 g
Protein . . . . 6 g

Baked Stuffed Shells or Manicotti

Preparation time: 25 minutes
Cooking time: 30 minutes
Serves: 6   Serving size: 1/6 recipe

Whichever pasta you choose, you'll appreciate that the richly flavored cheese filling has less than half the calories and fat of the original version. Like most baked pasta dishes, it can be made and refrigerated, covered, up to a day ahead.

8	oz jumbo shell pasta (28–30 pieces) or manicotti (12–14 pieces)
1	tsp olive oil
1/2	small onion, finely chopped
3	oz lean turkey ham, finely chopped
1	clove garlic, minced
1 1/2	cups part-skim ricotta cheese
1	10-oz pkg frozen chopped spinach, thawed and squeezed dry
1	cup shredded part-skim mozzarella cheese, divided
1	egg white, slightly beaten
1/2	tsp nutmeg
1	26-oz jar low-sodium tomato sauce (about 3 cups)
2	Tbsp grated Parmesan cheese

1. Cook the pasta according to package directions, omitting the salt. Drain, rinse well, and place in a large bowl (shells) or a large plate (manicotti).

2. Preheat the oven to 350°F. Spray a 9 × 13-inch baking pan with nonstick cooking spray.

3. Meanwhile, in a small nonstick skillet, heat the oil. Add the onion and ham; cook, stirring as needed, until the onion is translucent, about 3 minutes. Add the garlic and cook just until fragrant, about 30 seconds. Let cool.

4. In a large bowl, combine the ricotta, spinach, 1/2 cup mozzarella, egg white, and nutmeg; stir in the cooled onion mixture and blend thoroughly.

Exchanges
2 Starch
2 Lean Meat
2 Vegetable
1/2 Fat

Calories 349
  Calories from Fat . . 98
Total Fat . . . . 11 g
  Saturated Fat . . . . . . 6 g
Cholesterol . . . . 40 mg
Sodium . . . . 416 mg
Carbohydrate . . . . . . 42 g
  Dietary Fiber . . . . . . 4 g
  Sugars . . . . 6 g
Protein . . . . 23 g

5. With a small spoon, stuff the pasta shells or manicotti tubes with the ricotta mixture.

6. Spread about 1 cup of the tomato sauce in the prepared baking pan, then arrange the shells or manicotti evenly over the sauce. Top with the remaining sauce, sprinkle with the remaining 1/2 cup mozzarella and the Parmesan cheese, and bake until bubbly, 25–30 minutes.

Fettuccine Alfredo

Preparation time: 20 minutes
Cooking time: 15 minutes
Serves: 6   Serving size: 1 cup

This famous dish has been called a "heart attack on a plate," and no wonder. The original version combines a stick of butter, a cup of heavy cream, and loads of grated Parmesan cheese. We've cut the fat drastically by using flour as a thickener rather than cream. Another useful technique: bulking up the pasta portion with barely cooked thin zucchini strips, which look like fettuccine but contain only a fraction of the carbohydrates. If you have a vegetable slicer or mandoline, you can slice the zucchini to uniform paper-thinness. A little of our sauce goes a long way—and be sure to use a good-quality fresh Parmesan cheese, such as Parmegiano-Reggiano, for best flavor.

9	oz uncooked fettuccine pasta
1	medium zucchini, sliced into long, thin noodle-like strips
1	Tbsp unsalted butter or margarine
1	Tbsp all-purpose flour
3/4	cup low-fat (1%) milk
1/2	cup fresh grated Parmesan cheese
1	Tbsp fresh lemon juice
1/4	tsp nutmeg

1. Cook the pasta according to package directions, omitting the salt. In the last minute of cooking time, add the zucchini strips. Drain and place in a serving bowl; keep warm.

2. Meanwhile, in a medium nonstick skillet, melt the butter. Add the flour and cook, stirring constantly, until the mixture begins to turn a straw color, about 2 minutes (do not allow to burn). Remove from the heat and add the milk, whisking until smooth. Return to medium heat and cook, stirring frequently, until the mixture bubbles and begins to thicken, about 2 minutes. Add the cheese, lemon juice, and nutmeg; stir until smooth. Pour over the hot pasta and toss to coat. Serve immediately.

Exchanges
2 1/2 Starch
1 Fat

Calories 235
    Calories from Fat . . 58
Total Fat . . . . 6 g
    Saturated Fat . . . . . . 4 g
Cholesterol . . . . 54 mg
Sodium . . . . 87 mg
Carbohydrate . . . . . . 34 g
    Dietary Fiber . . . . . . 2 g
    Sugars . . . . 4 g
Protein . . . . 10 g

Lasagna

Preparation time: 20 minutes
Cooking time: 30 minutes
Serves: 8   Serving size: 1/8 recipe

It's amazing how fresh and delicious this lasagna tastes, with its well-seasoned meatballs and uncluttered Meaty Tomato Sauce (see recipe, p. 52). Using no-cook lasagna noodles saves time, but if you prefer the conventional type, just boil and drain them before proceeding with the recipe.

- 1 recipe Meaty Tomato Sauce (p. 52), prepared through step 3 (do not crumble the meatballs)
- 12 precooked lasagna noodles (about 8 oz)
- 2 cups part-skim ricotta cheese
- 2 10-oz pkg frozen chopped spinach, thawed and squeezed dry
- 2 cups shredded part-skim mozzarella cheese
- 4 Tbsp grated Parmesan cheese

1. Preheat the oven to 375°F. Spray a 9 × 13-inch baking pan with nonstick cooking spray.

2. Separate the tomato sauce from the meatballs, transferring the meatballs to a medium bowl. Crumble the meatballs with a wooden spoon or your hands.

3. Spread about 1 cup of the sauce in the prepared pan; arrange a layer of lasagna noodles over the sauce. Evenly scatter 1/3 of the crumbled meatballs on top, and, with a small spoon, dollops of 1/3 of the ricotta. Scatter 1/3 of the spinach over the top, then sprinkle evenly with 1/4 of the mozzarella cheese and dot with another cup of the sauce. Repeat, ending with the remaining lasagna noodles. Top evenly with the remaining meatballs, ricotta, spinach, and tomato sauce; sprinkle with the remaining mozzarella and the Parmesan cheese.

4. Cover with foil and bake until bubbling, about 20 minutes; remove the foil and bake until lightly browned along the edges, 10 minutes more. Let stand about 10 minutes before cutting.

Exchanges

2 1/2 Starch
3 Lean Meat
2 Vegetable
1/2 Fat

Calories 448
  Calories from Fat . 125
Total Fat . . . . 14 g
  Saturated Fat . . . . . . 8 g
Cholesterol . . . . 85 mg
Sodium . . . . 898 mg
Carbohydrate . . . . . . 49 g
  Dietary Fiber . . . . . . 6 g
  Sugars . . . . 11 g
Protein . . . . 33 g

Pizza Dough

Preparation time: 10 minutes
Resting time: 30 minutes
Serves: 8   Serving size: 1/8 pizza

Yes, it's more work to make your own pizza pie crust, but you'll never regret the effort. If you don't have a food processor, just make the recipe by hand. This practically foolproof recipe makes a flavorful, toothsome dough that leaves take-out pizza far behind. What's more, you can make the dough ahead of time and chill or freeze it, so all you need to do is assemble the toppings on your cooking day. Two techniques that make this crust wonderful are using bread flour instead of all-purpose, and stretching the dough rather than rolling it.

2 cups bread flour
1 envelope rapid-rise yeast
1/2 tsp salt
1 Tbsp olive oil

1. Spray a medium bowl and a 12-inch pizza pan or baking sheet with nonstick cooking spray.

2. In a food processor, combine the flour, yeast, and salt; pulse to blend.

3. In a glass measuring cup, combine 3/4 cup water and the oil; microwave on high until the water is very warm (120–130°F).

4. Turn the food processor on and continue blending the flour mixture; with the processor on, gradually pour the warm liquid through the feed tube. Process until the dough forms a ball, about 1 minute, then process 1 minute longer to knead.

5. Transfer the dough to the prepared bowl. Cover with a damp towel and allow to rest for 30 minutes. (The dough can be made ahead, wrapped in plastic, and refrigerated for up to 2 days, or frozen for up to 2 months.)

6. To shape the pizza, place the dough in the center of the prepared pizza pan, flattening it to a disk with the palm of your hand.

Exchanges
1 1/2 Starch
1/2 Fat

Calories 140
    Calories from Fat . . 19
Total Fat . . . . 2 g
    Saturated Fat . . . . . . 0 g
Cholesterol . . . . 0 mg
Sodium . . . . 146 mg
Carbohydrate . . . . . . 25 g
    Dietary Fiber . . . . . . 1 g
    Sugars . . . . 1 g
Protein . . . . 4 g

With your fingertips, push the dough from the center out to the edges, until it is 1/4 inch thick. Then place one hand over the center of the dough and with your other hand, stretch out one side of the dough. Rotate the dough a quarter turn; repeat until the dough is fully stretched to its full 12-inch diameter. (If the dough is too springy, cover it with a damp towel and let it rest 10 minutes, then try again.) Spray the dough with nonstick cooking spray before adding toppings to the pizza.

Hawaiian Pizza

Preparation time: 15 minutes
Cooking time: 15 minutes
Serves: 8   Serving size: 1/8 pizza

The red pepper, Roma tomatoes, pineapple, and Canadian bacon really make this pizza a full-flavored treat. The finished pizza is so colorful that you might want to cut it into 2-inch squares and serve it as an appetizer.

1 recipe Pizza Dough (p. 120)
1 Tbsp olive oil
2 red bell peppers, thinly sliced
3 Roma tomatoes, thinly sliced
6 slices Canadian bacon, cut into thin strips
1 tsp dried oregano
1 8-oz can crushed pineapple packed in water, drained
1 cup shredded part-skim mozzarella cheese

1. Place the oven rack on the lowest rung. Spray a 12-inch pizza pan or baking sheet with nonstick cooking spray. Preheat the oven to 450°F. Place the dough on the pan and spray with nonstick cooking spray.

2. In a medium skillet, heat the oil, add the peppers, and cook, stirring as needed until tender, about 1 minute. Stir in the tomatoes and cook 1 minute more. Add the bacon and oregano and toss to coat. Scatter the topping on the dough.

3. Bake 8 minutes, then sprinkle with the pineapple and cheese. Bake until the cheese melts and the crust is browned, about 5 minutes. Serve immediately.

Exchanges
2 Starch
1 Lean Meat
1 Vegetable
1/2 Fat

Calories 258
　Calories from Fat . . 71
Total Fat . . . . 8 g
　Saturated Fat . . . . . . 3 g
Cholesterol . . . . 20 mg
Sodium . . . . 545 mg
Carbohydrate . . . . . . 33 g
　Dietary Fiber . . . . . . 2 g
　Sugars . . . . 6 g
Protein . . . . 14 g

Pizza Margherita

Preparation time: 15 minutes
Cooking time: 15 minutes
Serves: 8   Serving size: 1/8 pizza

When it comes to pizza toppings, less is more. In this simple classic, the tomato sauce and cheese are added sparingly; this prevents the crust from getting heavy and soggy.

1	14-oz can crushed tomatoes in puree
1	Tbsp extra-virgin olive oil
1/2	tsp dried oregano
1	clove garlic, minced
1	recipe Pizza Dough (p. 120)
1	cup shredded part-skim mozzarella cheese
10–12	fresh basil leaves

1. Place the oven rack on the lowest rung. Spray a 12-inch pizza pan or baking sheet with nonstick cooking spray. Preheat the oven to 450°F.

2. To prepare the tomato sauce, in a small saucepan, combine the tomatoes, oil, oregano, and garlic; bring to a boil. Lower the heat and simmer 5 minutes; set aside.

3. Meanwhile, shape the pizza dough in the prepared pan as directed in the recipe. Spray with nonstick cooking spray.

4. Evenly spread the tomato sauce over the pizza. Bake until lightly browned, 10 minutes, then sprinkle with the cheese and basil leaves. Bake until bubbling, 5–8 minutes. Serve immediately.

Exchanges

2 Starch
1 Fat

Calories	206
Calories from Fat	54
Total Fat	6 g
Saturated Fat	2 g
Cholesterol	8 mg
Sodium	289 mg
Carbohydrate	29 g
Dietary Fiber	2 g
Sugars	2 g
Protein	9 g

Onion Pizza

Preparation time: 30 minutes
Cooking time: 15 minutes
Serves: 8   Serving size: 1/8 pizza

This richly flavored pizza makes a wonderful appetizer, too. Just bake in a 13 × 9-inch baking pan instead of a pizza pan, and cut into 32 pieces.

- 1 Tbsp extra-virgin olive oil
- 1 lb onions (4 medium), thinly sliced
- 1 Tbsp fresh rosemary leaves, or 1 tsp dried
- 1/4 tsp salt
  Fresh ground pepper to taste
- 1 recipe Pizza Dough (p. 120)
- 1/4 cup sliced black olives
- 2 Tbsp freshly grated Parmesan cheese

1. Place the oven rack on the lowest rung. Spray a 12-inch pizza pan or baking sheet with nonstick cooking spray. Preheat the oven to 450°F.

2. In a large nonstick skillet, heat the oil. Add the onions and cook, stirring as needed, until very soft and lightly browned, about 15 minutes. Sprinkle with the rosemary, salt, and pepper.

3. Meanwhile, shape the pizza dough in the prepared pan as directed in the recipe. Spray with nonstick cooking spray.

4. Scatter the onions evenly over the prepared crust. Top evenly with the olives. Bake until lightly browned, 8 minutes, then sprinkle with the cheese. Bake until the cheese melts and the crust is golden brown, 3–5 minutes. Serve immediately.

Exchanges
1 1/2 Starch
1 Vegetable
1 Fat

Calories 191
    Calories from Fat . . 49
Total Fat . . . . 5 g
    Saturated Fat . . . . . . 1 g
Cholesterol . . . . 1 mg
Sodium . . . . 289 mg
Carbohydrate . . . . . . 30 g
    Dietary Fiber . . . . . . 2 g
    Sugars . . . . 4 g
Protein . . . . 6 g

Sausage Pizza

Preparation time: 25 minutes
Cooking time: 15 minutes
Serves: 8   Serving size: 1/8 pizza

With a flavorful sausage topping, a little goes a long way—especially when it's thinned with meaty mushrooms and zucchini. To save even more fat, omit the turkey sausage and prepare your own by flavoring 1/4 lb lean ground turkey breast with a teaspoon each of fennel seed and freshly ground black pepper, then brown as directed in step 3.

1	14-oz can crushed tomatoes in puree
1	Tbsp extra-virgin olive oil
1/2	tsp dried oregano
1	clove garlic, minced
1/4	lb mild Italian-style turkey sausage, crumbled
1	cup diced fresh mushrooms
1/2	small zucchini, diced
1	recipe Pizza Dough (p. 120)
1	cup shredded part-skim mozzarella cheese

Exchanges

1 1/2 Starch
1 Very Lean Meat
1 Vegetable
1 Fat

Calories 233
 Calories from Fat . . 66
Total Fat . . . . 7 g
 Saturated Fat . . . . . . 3 g
Cholesterol . . . . 15 mg
Sodium . . . . 439 mg
Carbohydrate . . . . . . 30 g
 Dietary Fiber . . . . . . 2 g
 Sugars . . . . 3 g
Protein . . . . 11 g

1. Place the oven rack on the lowest rung. Spray a 12-inch pizza pan or baking sheet with nonstick cooking spray. Preheat the oven to 450°F.

2. To prepare the tomato sauce, in a small saucepan, combine the tomatoes, oil, oregano, and garlic; bring to a boil. Lower the heat and simmer 5 minutes; set aside.

3. Spray a medium nonstick skillet with nonstick cooking spray; heat. Add the sausage and cook, stirring, until well browned, 3–4 minutes; transfer with a slotted spoon to a plate. Drain off the accumulated fat and return the pan to the heat. Add the mushrooms and zucchini; cook, stirring, until the mushrooms have released and reabsorbed their juices and the zucchini is lightly browned, about 5 minutes; set aside.

4. Meanwhile, shape the pizza dough in the prepared pan as directed in the recipe. Spray with nonstick cooking spray.

5. Evenly spread the tomato sauce over the pizza. Bake until lightly browned, 10 minutes, then sprinkle with the sausage, cooked vegetables, and cheese. Bake until bubbling, 5–8 minutes. Serve immediately.

Rigatoni Primavera

Preparation time: 15 minutes
Cooking time: none
Serves: 8   Serving size: 1 3/4 cups

The idea behind this recipe is to cook enough pasta so everyone can have a cup of pasta and 3/4 cup vegetables. Fresh vegetables that are steamed just until they are tender will give you the richest colors and textures, but feel free to use frozen vegetables for convenience. You can easily slice the vegetables while the pasta water heats.

1	lb rigatoni pasta
1	Tbsp olive oil
1	tsp minced garlic
1/2	large onion, diced
1	cup yellow or zucchini squash, sliced 1/4 inch thick
1	cup broccoli flowerets
1/2	green bell pepper, cut in strips
1	large tomato, seeded and cut into 8 wedges
2	Tbsp minced fresh basil (about 5 leaves), diced
1/2	cup grated Parmesan cheese
1/4	cup crumbled feta cheese

1. Cook the rigatoni according to package directions, omitting the salt. Drain and place in a serving bowl; keep warm.

2. Meanwhile, place the oil and garlic in a large skillet and heat until just sizzling. Add the onion and cook until softened, 2 minutes. Add the squash, broccoli, and green pepper and cook on low heat, stirring occasionally, until tender, about 5–6 minutes. Stir in the tomato and basil; cook until heated through, about 2 minutes. Remove from the heat; cover and keep warm.

3. Sprinkle the cooked rigatoni with half of the Parmesan cheese; top with the cooked vegetables and sprinkle with remaining Parmesan and feta cheeses. Serve immediately.

Exchanges
3 Starch
1 Vegetable

Calories	281
Calories from Fat	50
Total Fat	6 g
Saturated Fat	2 g
Cholesterol	11 mg
Sodium	176 mg
Carbohydrate	47 g
Dietary Fiber	3 g
Sugars	4 g
Protein	12 g

Spaghetti with Meatballs

Preparation time: 25 minutes
Cooking time: 2 hours
Serves: 6   Serving: 1/6 recipe

The Meaty Tomato Sauce from p. 52 makes about 6 cups of sauce. Only 3 cups are used in this recipe. Use the extra as a wonderful topping for cooked vegetables, prebaked pizza crust, or another pasta meal. You can refrigerate it, covered, for up to 4 days, or freeze up to 3 months. If you prefer no leftovers, use only half a can (about 2 cups) each of the diced tomatoes and crushed tomatoes called for in the Meaty Tomato Sauce recipe.

> 1 recipe Meaty Tomato Sauce (p. 52), prepared up to step 3 (do not crumble the meatballs)
>
> 9 oz spaghetti or other pasta

1. Cook the pasta according to package directions, omitting the salt. Drain and place in a serving bowl.

2. Top with 3 cups of the sauce and the 12 meatballs (reserve the remaining sauce for another use).

Exchanges

2 1/2 Starch
1 Very Lean Meat
2 Vegetable

Calories 296
  Calories from Fat . . 36
Total Fat . . . . 4 g
  Saturated Fat . . . . . . 1 g
Cholesterol . . . . 62 mg
Sodium . . . . 458 mg
Carbohydrate . . . . . . 46 g
  Dietary Fiber . . . . . . 4 g
  Sugars . . . . 7 g
Protein . . . . 19 g

Spaghetti Carbonara

Preparation time: 15 minutes
Cooking time: 20 minutes
Serves: 8   Serving size: 1 cup

This carbonara dish serves as a tasty alternative to the popular creamy version. As you prepare it, enjoy the delicious smell of bacon sizzling on the stove.

- 1 lb spaghetti
- 1/2 lb bacon, diced
- 1 egg, lightly beaten
- 3/4 cup grated Parmesan or Pecorino Romano cheese
- 2 Tbsp low-fat (1%) milk
- 1 garlic clove, minced
  Dash ground black pepper

1. Cook the spaghetti according to package directions. Drain and keep warm.

2. Meanwhile, in a large skillet on medium-high, cook the bacon until crisp, 6–8 minutes. Drain on a paper towel-lined plate.

3. In a medium bowl, whisk together the egg, cheese, milk, garlic, and pepper to a thick paste. Stir into the hot, cooked spaghetti and toss until the egg begins to cook. Place in a microwavable serving dish and microwave on high until the egg is fully cooked, 45–60 seconds. Remove and top with bacon pieces. Serve immediately.

Exchanges

3 Starch
1 Lean Meat
1/2 Fat

Calories 312
  Calories from Fat . . 81
Total Fat . . . . 9 g
  Saturated Fat . . . . . . 4 g
Cholesterol . . . . 45 mg
Sodium . . . . 330 mg
Carbohydrate . . . . . . 43 g
  Dietary Fiber . . . . . . 2 g
  Sugars . . . . 3 g
Protein . . . . 15 g

Serve with baby carrots or carrot sticks, or a crisp salad with a variety of leafy greens (try spinach, arugula, radicchio, or baby Swiss chard). The bitterness of the greens complements the rich carbonara beautifully.

Spaghetti Carbonara, Creamy Version

Preparation time: 15 minutes
Cooking time: 20 minutes
Serves: 6   Serving size: 1/6 recipe

This is one of those dishes that makes the most out of a few classic ingredients: pancetta (Italian bacon), eggs, fresh grated cheese, and pasta. By using lean Canadian bacon and substituting cottage cheese for some of the eggs, we've kept the simplicity of the original version without losing its divine flavor and creaminess. Be sure to use imported cheese and grate it yourself—the extra flavor of Pecorino Romano (made from sheep's milk instead of cow's milk) is well worth it! To offset the creamy pasta, serve with crisp vegetables in a sour dressing—like tender-crisp beets or asparagus tossed with vinaigrette, or a cucumber-tomato salad.

> 9   oz spaghetti
> 2   eggs
> 1/2 cup low-fat (1%) cottage cheese
> 2   Tbsp extra-virgin olive oil
> 3   oz Canadian bacon, finely diced
> 1/3 cup fresh grated Romano cheese

1. Cook the spaghetti according to package directions. Drain and keep warm.

2. Meanwhile, in a food processor or blender, puree the eggs and cottage cheese until smooth; set aside.

3. In a large nonstick skillet, heat the oil. Cook the bacon until well browned, about 4 minutes. Add the hot cooked pasta, the egg mixture, and the Romano cheese; toss in the pan until the eggs are cooked through, about 3 minutes. Serve immediately.

Exchanges
2 1/2 Starch
1 Lean Meat
1/2 Fat

Calories 279
  Calories from Fat . . 85
Total Fat . . . . 9 g
  Saturated Fat . . . . . . 3 g
Cholesterol . . . . 85 mg
Sodium . . . . 351 mg
Carbohydrate . . . . . . 33 g
  Dietary Fiber . . . . . . 1 g
  Sugars . . . . 3 g
Protein . . . . 15 g

Quick Breads & Muffins

Recipes

Banana Bread

Preparation time: 15 minutes
Cooking time: 50–60 minutes
Serves: 16   Serving size: 1 slice

Cooks who long ago mashed bananas for traditional banana bread were way ahead of their time. Recently, other fruits such as pureed prunes, apples, and apricots have also been used as fat replacers to decrease the recipe's fat content.

1 1/2 cup all-purpose flour
1 tsp baking soda
1/2 tsp salt
1/2 tsp ground allspice
2/3 cup low-fat (1%) milk
1/2 cup firmly packed light brown sugar
1/3 cup vegetable oil
1 egg
1 egg white
1 tsp vanilla extract
1 cup mashed banana (about 3 6-inch bananas)

1. Preheat the oven to 350°F. Spray a 9 × 5-inch loaf pan with nonstick spray.

2. In a medium bowl, whisk together the flour, baking soda, salt, and allspice. Make a well in the center.

3. In another medium bowl, combine the milk, sugar, oil, egg, egg white, and vanilla until well blended, removing any lumps. Stir in the banana. Pour into the well in the flour mixture; stir just to combine (do not over-mix), about 1 minute. Pour the batter into the prepared pan.

4. Bake until a toothpick inserted in the center comes out clean, 50–60 minutes; avoid underbaking. Cool in the pan on a rack, 5–10 minutes, then remove from the pan and place on the rack to finish cooling.

Exchanges
1 1/2 Carbohydrate
1/2 Fat

Calories 134
    Calories from Fat . . 48
Total Fat . . . . 5 g
    Saturated Fat . . . . . . 0 g
Cholesterol . . . . 14 mg
Sodium . . . . 167 mg
Carbohydrate . . . . . . 20 g
    Dietary Fiber . . . . . . 1 g
    Sugars . . . . 10 g
Protein . . . . 2 g

Buttermilk Biscuits

Preparation time: 15 minutes
Cooking time: 15–20 minutes
Serves: 8   Serving size: 1 biscuit

The secret to these tender, flaky biscuits is keeping things cool and working quickly. Make sure the butter is thoroughly chilled and cut into tiny pieces so you can blend it quickly.

1 1/2 cups all-purpose flour
1 tsp baking powder
1/2 tsp salt
3 Tbsp chilled unsalted butter or stick margarine, cut into small pieces
2/3 cup chilled low-fat (1%) buttermilk
2 tsp fat-free (skim) milk

1. Preheat the oven to 400°F. Spray a baking sheet with nonstick cooking spray.

2. In a bowl, whisk together the flour, baking powder, and salt. Using a pastry blender or 2 knives, cut in the butter until the mixture forms coarse crumbs. With a fork, stir in the buttermilk just until evenly moistened.

3. Turn the dough out onto a lightly floured surface; knead lightly 4 times. Pat the dough to 1/2-inch thickness and cut with a 2-inch round biscuit cutter to make 8 biscuits. Place on the prepared baking sheet, brush the tops lightly with the milk, and bake until lightly browned and puffy, 15–20 minutes.

Exchanges
1 Carbohydrate
1 Fat

Calories 132
    Calories from Fat . . 42
Total Fat . . . . 5 g
    Saturated Fat . . . . . . 3 g
Cholesterol . . . . 12 mg
Sodium . . . . 214 mg
Carbohydrate . . . . . . 19 g
    Dietary Fiber . . . . . . 1 g
    Sugars . . . . 1 g
Protein . . . . 3 g

Chive Biscuits

Preparation time: 15 minutes
Cooking time: 15 minutes
Serves: 8   Serving size: 1 biscuit

Think biscuits have to be loaded with butter to taste good? Think again! This recipe uses margarine and chives for a wonderful flavor.

> 1 cup all-purpose flour
> 1 tsp baking powder
> 1/4 tsp salt
> 3 Tbsp stick margarine
> 2 Tbsp fresh chives, chopped
> 1/3 cup low-fat buttermilk
> 1 Tbsp low-fat (1%) milk

1. Preheat the oven to 400°F. Line a baking sheet with parchment paper or spray with nonstick cooking spray.

2. In a medium bowl, whisk the flour, baking powder, and salt until blended. Cut in the margarine with a pastry blender or 2 knives until the mixture resembles coarse crumbs, 2–3 minutes. Add the chives and stir to blend. Add the buttermilk; stir until just combined (do not over-mix).

3. Turn the dough onto a lightly floured surface and knead 3–4 times. Flatten the dough to about 1/2 inch thick. Using a 2-inch biscuit cutter, cut out biscuits and place on the prepared baking sheet. With a pastry brush, brush the tops of the biscuits lightly with the milk.

4. Bake until lightly browned, about 15 minutes.

Exchanges
1 Starch
1/2 Fat

Calories 100
　Calories from Fat . . 41
Total Fat . . . . 5 g
　Saturated Fat . . . . . . 1 g
Cholesterol . . . . 0 mg
Sodium . . . . 180 mg
Carbohydrate . . . . . . 13 g
　Dietary Fiber . . . . . . 0 g
　Sugars . . . . 1 g
Protein . . . . 2 g

Cinnamon Coffee Cake

Preparation time: 12 minutes
Cooking time: 18–20 minutes
Serves: 12   Serving size: 1 slice

This attractive coffee cake is made in a bundt pan and wows the eater with its impressive center cinnamon and chocolate swirl.

Cake
- 1 1/4 cups all-purpose flour
- 1 1/4 tsp baking powder
- 1/4 tsp salt
- 5 Tbsp stick margarine
- 1/3 cup granulated sugar
- 1 1/2 tsp vanilla extract
- 2 eggs
- 1/4 cup low-fat (1%) milk

Swirl
- 1 1/2 tsp cinnamon
- 1 1/2 tsp unsweetened cocoa powder
- 1 tsp granulated sugar

1. Preheat the oven to 350°F. Spray a 12-cup bundt pan with nonstick cooking spray.

2. In a medium bowl, whisk the flour, baking powder, and salt. Set aside.

3. In a medium bowl, with an electric mixer at medium speed, beat the margarine until creamy, 1–2 minutes. Gradually blend in the sugar. Add the vanilla and eggs, stirring until smooth. Add the flour mixture alternately with the milk, ending with flour. Stir 1 more minute.

4. In a small bowl, mix the cinnamon, cocoa, and sugar together until blended.

5. Sprinkle 1 tsp of the cinnamon mixture into the bottom of the prepared bundt pan. Spread half of the batter on top. Sprinkle with 1 1/2 tsp of the cinnamon mixture; top with the remaining batter, then the remaining

Exchanges
1 Carbohydrate
1 Fat

Calories 127
  Calories from Fat . . 52
Total Fat . . . . 6 g
  Saturated Fat . . . . . . 1 g
Cholesterol . . . . 36 mg
Sodium . . . . 155 mg
Carbohydrate . . . . . . 16 g
  Dietary Fiber . . . . . . 0 g
  Sugars . . . . 6 g
Protein . . . . 3 g

cinnamon mixture. To swirl, take a knife and cut through the entire batter, swerving the knife back and forth.

6. Bake until a toothpick inserted in the center comes out clean, about 18–20 minutes. Cool in the pan for 10 minutes, then invert onto a plate. If needed, loosen the cake with a knife before inverting.

Cinnamon Doughnuts

Preparation time: 25 minutes
Cooking time: 7–10 minutes per batch
Serves: 18   Serving size: 2 doughnuts

These tasty morsels require a mini-doughnut pan (available at kitchen supply stores) and a little ingenuity. They illustrate a helpful principle when cutting carbohydrates: make the most of just a little sugar. Here, the doughnuts are only lightly sweetened, but a thin glaze and a sprinkle of crunchy cinnamon sugar on top gives maximum sweetness impact.

Doughnuts
1 1/2 cups all-purpose flour
    2 tsp baking powder
    2 Tbsp cinnamon
  1/4 tsp salt
  1/8 tsp nutmeg
    1 Tbsp unsalted butter
  1/2 cup low-fat (1%) milk
  1/3 cup granulated sugar
    1 egg
    1 Tbsp canola oil
    1 tsp vanilla extract

Glaze
    2 Tbsp granulated sugar
  1/2 tsp cinnamon
  1/4 cup powdered sugar
1 1/2–2 tsp hot water

1. Preheat the oven to 350°F. Spray a mini-doughnut pan with nonstick cooking spray.

2. Sift together the flour, baking powder, cinnamon, salt, and nutmeg onto a sheet of wax paper.

3. In a medium saucepan over low heat, melt the butter and continue cooking, stirring gently, until golden brown and fragrant, 3–4 minutes (do not allow to burn). Remove from the heat and whisk in the milk, sugar, egg, oil, and vanilla until smooth, 1 minute. Gradually add the flour mixture, beating until well blended.

Exchanges
1 Carbohydrate

Calories 83
    Calories from Fat . . 17
Total Fat . . . . 2 g
    Saturated Fat . . . . . . 1 g
Cholesterol . . . . 14 mg
Sodium . . . . 80 mg
Carbohydrate . . . . . . 15 g
    Dietary Fiber . . . . . . 0 g
    Sugars . . . . 7 g
Protein . . . . 2 g

4. Spoon the dough into a large pastry bag fitted with a 1/4-inch tip. Pipe 1/3 of the dough into the molds of the prepared pan, filling them about 2/3 full. Bake until springy to the touch, about 7–10 minutes. Set on a rack to cool slightly. Repeat with the remaining dough.

5. Meanwhile, prepare the glaze: in a small bowl, combine the granulated sugar and cinnamon; set aside.

6. In another small bowl, combine the powdered sugar with 1 1/2 tsp of the hot water, adding a little more water as needed, until you have a thin glaze. Brush a thin layer of glaze onto the top of each still-warm doughnut; sprinkle each immediately with a little of the cinnamon-sugar mixture. Serve warm.

If you don't have a pastry bag, use a zippered plastic bag and cut off a bottom corner equal to 1/4 inch.

Cinnamon Rolls

Preparation time: 40 minutes
Standing time: 1 hour
Cooking time: 12–15 minutes
Serves: 16   Serving size: 1 roll

No one will suspect these sticky sweet rolls have a fraction of the fat and sugar of the originals. They're best served warm, with a cup of hot coffee.

Dough
1 Tbsp packed light brown sugar
1 Tbsp cinnamon
1/2 cup warm water (105–115°F)
1 package (2 1/4 tsp) active dry yeast
3/4 cup warm fat-free (skim) milk (105–115°F)
4 cups all-purpose flour
1 large egg, lightly beaten
1/4 cup granulated sugar
2 Tbsp canola oil
1 tsp salt

Icing
1/2 cup powdered sugar
1 Tbsp reduced-fat brick-style cream cheese
1 tsp vanilla extract
1 tsp water

1. Preheat the oven to 400°F. Spray a 13 × 9-inch baking dish with nonstick cooking spray.

2. In a small bowl, combine the brown sugar and cinnamon; set aside.

3. Combine the warm water and yeast in a large mixing bowl and let stand until the yeast is dissolved, about 5 minutes.

4. Stir the warm milk into the yeast mixture. Add 1 cup of the flour and the egg, sugar, oil, and salt; stir until well blended. Add remaining flour, 1/2 cup at a time, until dough becomes very stiff.

Exchanges
2 Carbohydrate

Calories 171
    Calories from Fat . . 23
Total Fat . . . . 3 g
    Saturated Fat . . . . . . 0 g
Cholesterol . . . . 14 mg
Sodium . . . . 160 mg
Carbohydrate . . . . . . 32 g
    Dietary Fiber . . . . . . 1 g
    Sugars . . . . 8 g
Protein . . . . 4 g

5. Turn the dough out onto a lightly floured work surface and knead until smooth and elastic, about 10 minutes.

6. Roll the dough out into a 12 × 18-inch rectangle. Sprinkle evenly with the brown sugar-cinnamon mixture. Starting from one long side, roll up the dough as you would a jelly roll. Cut crosswise into 16 slices.

7. Place the rolls, cut side up, slightly apart in the prepared dish. Cover with plastic wrap and let rise in a warm place until doubled in volume, about 1 hour.

8. Bake 12–15 minutes, or until browned. Invert pan onto prepared platter and let cool.

9. In a small bowl, combine the powdered sugar, cream cheese, vanilla, and water. Stir until creamy and spread evenly over the warm rolls.

Date Nut Bread

Preparation time: 15 minutes
Cooking time: 35 minutes
Serves: 16   Serving size: 1 slice

Have you been avoiding dates? This could be the bread for you! It's moist, nutty, and low in fat.

1/2 cup diced dried dates
1/2 cup water
  1 cup all-purpose flour
1/2 cup whole-wheat flour
  2 Tbsp chopped walnuts
  1 tsp baking powder
  1 tsp cinnamon
  1 tsp ground nutmeg
1/4 tsp salt
3/4 cup firmly packed dark brown sugar
1/2 cup low-fat (1%) milk
1/4 cup vegetable oil
  1 egg
  1 tsp vanilla extract
  1 tsp granulated sugar, for topping

Exchanges
1 1/2 Carbohydrate
1 Fat

Calories 142
  Calories from Fat . . 42
Total Fat . . . . 5 g
  Saturated Fat . . . . . . 0 g
Cholesterol . . . . 14 mg
Sodium . . . . 71 mg
Carbohydrate . . . . . . 24 g
  Dietary Fiber . . . . . . 1 g
  Sugars . . . . 14 g
Protein . . . . 2 g

1. Preheat the oven to 350°F. Spray a 9 × 5-inch loaf pan with nonstick spray.

2. Place the dried dates and water in a small saucepan; heat over medium heat until the water simmers; reduce the heat to low and simmer, 2 minutes. Remove from the heat and set aside.

3. In a medium bowl, whisk together the flours, walnuts, baking powder, cinnamon, nutmeg, and salt. Make a well in the center.

4. In another medium bowl, stir together the brown sugar, milk, oil, egg, and vanilla until well blended. Pour into the well of the flour mixture; stir just until combined (do not over-mix), about 1 minute. Pour the batter into the prepared pan.

5. Bake until a toothpick inserted in the center comes out clean, about 35 minutes. Cool in the pan on a rack, 5–10 minutes, then remove from the pan and place on the rack to finish cooling.

Blueberry Muffins

Preparation time: 15 minutes
Cooking time: 15–18 minutes
Serves: 18   Serving size: 1 muffin

Fresh or frozen blueberries work equally well in this recipe. Enjoy these delicious muffins at any meal or as a snack.

2	cups all-purpose flour
2/3	cup granulated sugar
1	Tbsp baking powder
1/2	tsp baking soda
1/4	tsp salt
1/4	cup vegetable oil
1	egg
1	cup low-fat (1%) milk
1	Tbsp vanilla extract
1	cup fresh or frozen blueberries

1. Preheat the oven to 350°F. Spray 18 cups of 2 12-cup muffin tins with nonstick cooking spray or line with paper liners.

2. In medium bowl, whisk together the flour, sugar, baking powder, baking soda, and salt until well blended, about 1 minute.

3. In another medium bowl, combine the oil, egg, milk, and vanilla until well blended. Pour this liquid mixture into the middle of the flour mixture; stir until not quite all combined. Add the blueberries and gently finish combining. Spoon the batter into the cups, filling each about 2/3 full.

4. Bake until a toothpick inserted in the center comes out clean, about 15–18 minutes. Cool in the tins on a rack, 5 minutes, then remove from pan and place on the rack to finish cooling.

Exchanges
1 1/2 Carbohydrate
1 Fat

Calories	142
Calories from Fat	. . 42
Total Fat	5 g
Saturated Fat	0 g
Cholesterol	14 mg
Sodium	71 mg
Carbohydrate	24 g
Dietary Fiber	1 g
Sugars	14 g
Protein	2 g

Since this recipe makes 18 muffins and most muffin tins have 12 cups, simply leave 6 cups empty on one of the tins and fill them halfway with water.

Lemon Poppyseed Muffins

Preparation time: 15 minutes
Cooking time: 18–20 minutes
Serves: 18   Serving size: 1 muffin

These muffins have become favorites in the mini-muffin business. You'll love our low-fat version.

    2   cups all-purpose flour
  2/3   cup granulated sugar
    2   Tbsp poppy seeds
    1   Tbsp baking powder
  1/2   tsp baking soda
  1/4   tsp salt
    8   oz fat-free lemon yogurt
  1/4   cup vegetable oil
    1   egg
    1   Tbsp low-fat (1%) milk
    1   Tbsp vanilla extract
    1   Tbsp lemon zest

1. Preheat the oven to 350°F. Spray 18 cups of 2 12-cup muffin tins with nonstick cooking spray or line with paper liners.

2. In a medium bowl, whisk together the flour, sugar, poppyseeds, baking powder, baking soda, and salt until well blended. Make a well in the center.

3. In another medium bowl, combine the oil, egg, milk, yogurt, vanilla, and zest until well blended. Pour into the well in the flour mixture; stir just until combined (do not over-mix), about 1 minute. Spoon the batter into the cups, filling each about 2/3 full.

4. Bake until a toothpick inserted in the center comes out clean, 15–18 minutes. Cool in the tins on a rack, 5 minutes, then remove from the pan and place on the rack to finish cooling.

Exchanges

1 1/2 Carbohydrate
1/2 Fat

Calories 123
    Calories from Fat . . 36
Total Fat . . . . 4 g
    Saturated Fat . . . . . . 0 g
Cholesterol . . . . 12 mg
Sodium . . . . 140 mg
Carbohydrate . . . . . . 20 g
    Dietary Fiber . . . . . . 0 g
    Sugars . . . . 8 g
Protein . . . . 2 g

Since this recipe makes 18 muffins and most muffin tins have 12 cups, simply leave 6 cups empty on one of the tins and fill them halfway with water.

Zucchini Bread

Preparation time: 15 minutes
Cooking time: 55 minutes
Serves: 16 Serving size: 1 slice

Zucca is Italian for gourd, but zucchini are considered an abundant summer squash to most of us. Small or medium zucchini are ideal for baking because they are more tender. This bread is always a favorite; even when made with less oil and sugar, its taste isn't compromised at all.

2	cups all-purpose flour
1/2	tsp salt
1/2	tsp baking powder
1/2	tsp baking soda
2	tsp cinnamon
3/4	cup firmly packed light brown sugar
6	Tbsp canola oil
1/4	cup low-fat (1%) milk
2	eggs
2	tsp vanilla extract
3	small or 2 medium unpeeled zucchini, grated (about 2 cups)
2	tsp granulated sugar

1. Preheat the oven to 350°F. Spray a 9 × 5-inch loaf pan with nonstick cooking spray.

2. In a medium bowl, whisk the flour, salt, baking powder, baking soda, and cinnamon.

3. In another medium bowl, with an electric mixer at medium speed, beat the brown sugar, oil, milk, eggs, and vanilla until well blended, about 1 minute. Add the zucchini and continue beating 1 minute more. Let the mixture stand for 5 minutes. Stir in the flour mixture until just combined (do not over-mix), about 1 minute. Pour into the prepared loaf pan.

4. Sprinkle the top of the batter with the granulated sugar and bake until a toothpick inserted in the center comes out clean, about 55 minutes. Cool in the pan on a rack, 5–10 minutes, then remove from the pan and place on the rack to finish cooling.

Exchanges

1 1/2 Carbohydrate
1 Fat

Calories 159	
Calories from Fat . . 55	
Total Fat . . . . 6 g	
Saturated Fat . . . . . . 0 g	
Cholesterol . . . . 27 mg	
Sodium . . . . 138 mg	
Carbohydrate . . . . . . 23 g	
Dietary Fiber . . . . . . 1 g	
Sugars . . . . 11 g	
Protein . . . . 3 g	

Raisin Scones

Preparation time: 18 minutes
Cooking time: 15–20 minutes
Serves: 12   Serving size: 1 scone

Don't be scared off by the number of ingredients in these scones; the preparation is quite simple. And, the result is a delicious low-fat, low-sugar scone that still tastes quite rich and sweet. We found scone recipes that contained 20 grams of fat in one scone; that's 5 times the amount here!

1/3	cup seedless raisins
1	Tbsp firmly packed light brown sugar
1	tsp cinnamon
2	cups all-purpose flour
1/4	cup granulated sugar
2	tsp baking powder
1/2	tsp baking soda
1/2	tsp salt
1/8	tsp nutmeg
4	Tbsp stick margarine
1	egg
1 1/2	tsp vanilla extract
2/3	cup plain fat-free yogurt
1	tsp granulated sugar
1/4	tsp cinnamon

1. Preheat the oven to 400°F. Spray a baking sheet with nonstick cooking spray.

2. In a small bowl, combine the raisins, brown sugar, and cinnamon and stir to blend. Set aside.

3. In a medium bowl, whisk together the flour, granulated sugar, baking powder, baking soda, salt, and nutmeg. Cut in the margarine with a pastry blender or 2 knives until the mixture resembles coarse crumbs. Set aside.

4. In another small bowl, whisk the egg until frothy. Add the vanilla and yogurt and whisk together until smooth and creamy, about 1 minute.

Exchanges
2 Carbohydrate
1/2 Fat

Calories 156
  Calories from Fat . . 40
Total Fat . . . . 4 g
  Saturated Fat . . . . . . 1 g
Cholesterol . . . . 18 mg
Sodium . . . . 271 mg
Carbohydrate . . . . . . 26 g
  Dietary Fiber . . . . . . 1 g
  Sugars . . . . 9 g
Protein . . . . 4 g

5. Add the egg and yogurt mixture to the flour mixture and stir with a wooden spoon until the mixture leaves the sides of the bowl. Continue stirring 1 more minute; the dough will be sticky. Add the raisin mixture and stir until the raisins are spread throughout the dough, about 1 minute.

6. Coat your hands with nonstick cooking spray and place the dough onto the prepared baking sheet. Form the dough into an 8-inch circle, about 3/4 inch to 1 inch thick. Using a sharp knife, cut the dough into 12 equal wedges; separate the wedges slightly, about 1/4 inch apart.

7. To make the topping, combine the sugar and cinnamon, then sprinkle evenly over the dough.

8. Bake until browned, 15–20 minutes. Serve warm.

Cookies & Bars

Recipes

Apricot Bars

Preparation time: 8 minutes
Cooking time: 18–20 minutes
Serves: 20   Serving size: 1 bar

This recipe replaces most of the fat with an apricot puree that you can easily make in your blender or food processor. After you puree the apricots, add the other ingredients and mix. The lemon zest really enhances the apricots and these bars burst with sweet flavor.

- 3/4 cup dried apricots, divided
- 1/3 cup water
- 3/4 cup all-purpose flour
- 1 tsp baking powder
- 3/4 tsp cinnamon
- 1/4 tsp baking soda
- 1 egg
- 1/2 cup granulated sugar
- 1 Tbsp canola oil
- 1 Tbsp grated lemon zest
- 1 tsp vanilla
- 2 tsp powdered sugar

1. Preheat the oven to 350°F. Spray an 8 × 8-inch baking pan with nonstick cooking spray.

2. In a small saucepan, simmer 1/2 cup of the apricots in the water, covered, for 2 minutes. Cool, but do not drain. In a small bowl, dice the remaining apricots.

3. Meanwhile, in a medium bowl, whisk together the flour, baking powder, cinnamon, and baking soda. Stir in the diced apricots.

4. In a blender, add the cooled apricot mixture and puree, about 1 minute. Add the egg, granulated sugar, oil, zest, and vanilla and mix until just blended, about 30 seconds. Pour this mixture into the middle of the flour mixture and stir until just combined. Spread in the prepared pan and bake until golden brown and edges begin to crust, 18–20 minutes.

5. Sprinkle powdered sugar over the warm bars. Cool before cutting.

Exchanges
1 Carbohydrate

Calories	59
Calories from Fat	9
Total Fat	1 g
Saturated Fat	0 g
Cholesterol	11 mg
Sodium	38 mg
Carbohydrate	12 g
Dietary Fiber	1 g
Sugars	7 g
Protein	1 g

You can place the apricot squares in decorative mini-muffin liners to serve.

Blonde Brownies

Preparation time: 8 minutes
Cooking time: 20 minutes
Serves: 16   Serving size: 1 brownie

Hard to believe something so yummy could be this easy. Simply melt the margarine and stir in the other ingredients.

1/3 cup stick margarine
3/4 cup firmly packed light brown sugar
  1 egg, slightly beaten
  1 tsp vanilla extract
1/2 tsp baking powder
1/8 tsp baking soda
  1 cup all-purpose flour
1/4 cup mini-chocolate chips

1. Preheat the oven to 350°F. Spray an 8 × 8-inch baking pan with nonstick cooking spray.

2. In a medium saucepan, melt the margarine. Add the sugar and stir until smooth and slightly cooked, 2 minutes. Blend in the egg. Add the vanilla, baking powder, and baking soda; stir just to remove lumps. Add the flour and stir smooth. Stir in the chocolate chips.

3. Spread the batter in the prepared baking pan. Bake until the top is slightly set and lightly browned, 20 minutes; do not over-bake.

Exchanges
1 Carbohydrate
1 Fat

Calories 119
   Calories from Fat . . 45
Total Fat . . . . 5 g
   Saturated Fat . . . . . . 1 g
Cholesterol . . . . 13 mg
Sodium . . . . 74 mg
Carbohydrate . . . . . . 18 g
   Dietary Fiber . . . . . . 0 g
   Sugars . . . . 12 g
Protein . . . . 1 g

Chewy Granola Bars

Preparation time: 18 minutes
Cooking time: 20 minutes
Serves: 9   Serving size: 1 bar

These granola bars are moist and chewy, making them a wonderful treat. Try them in the kids' lunchboxes. They'll keep in an airtight container up to 1 week, or in the freezer up to 2 months.

1	cup old-fashioned rolled oats
1/3	cup orange juice
1	egg
1/4	cup honey
1/4	cup creamy peanut butter
1	Tbsp mini chocolate chips

1. Preheat the oven to 350°F. Spray an 8 × 8-inch square baking pan with nonstick cooking spray.

2. In a medium bowl, combine the oats, orange juice, egg, and honey. Let sit for 10 minutes to soften the oats.

3. Stir in the peanut butter and chocolate chips until blended. Spread in the pan. Bake until the top begins to firm, about 20 minutes. Cool for 10 minutes before cutting.

Exchanges
1 Carbohydrate
1 Fat

Calories 124
    Calories from Fat . . 46
Total Fat . . . . 5 g
    Saturated Fat . . . . . . 1 g
Cholesterol . . . . 24 mg
Sodium . . . . 41 mg
Carbohydrate . . . . . . 17 g
    Dietary Fiber . . . . . . 1 g
    Sugars . . . . 10 g
Protein . . . . 4 g

Gingerbread People

Preparation time: 30 minutes
Freezing time: 1 hour
Cooking time: 7–10 minutes
Serves: 36   Serving size: 1 cookie

Intensely fragrant and slightly spicy, this holiday staple loses nothing when both sugar and fat are reduced. The secret: prune puree, whose smooth texture substitutes for much of the fat and whose flavor complements the gingerbread spices. You can make your own (see below) or use prepared prune puree found in the baking or dried fruit aisles of most supermarkets. Keep the gingerbread men in an airtight container for 2 weeks; in the freezer, 2 months.

Gingerbread People
3	cups bleached all-purpose flour
1	Tbsp ground ginger
2	tsp cinnamon
1 1/2	tsp baking powder
1/2	tsp baking soda
1/2	tsp ground cloves
1/4	tsp salt
1/4	cup canola oil
1/4	cup prune puree
3	Tbsp unsalted butter or stick margarine, softened
1/3	cup firmly packed dark brown sugar
1	egg
1/2	cup dark molasses
2	tsp vanilla extract
1	tsp grated orange or lemon zest

Icing
1	cup powdered sugar
2–2 1/2	Tbsp hot water
1/8	tsp vanilla, orange, or lemon extract
1–2	drops food coloring (optional)

1. In a large bowl, whisk together the flour, ginger, cinnamon, baking powder, baking soda, cloves, and salt; set aside.

Exchanges
1 Carbohydrate
1/2 Fat

Calories 99
  Calories from Fat . . 25
Total Fat . . . . 3 g
  Saturated Fat . . . . . . 1 g
Cholesterol . . . . 8 mg
Sodium . . . . 54 mg
Carbohydrate . . . . . . 17 g
  Dietary Fiber . . . . . . 0 g
  Sugars . . . . 8 g
Protein . . . . 1 g

2. In a medium bowl with an electric mixer, combine the oil, prune puree, butter, brown sugar, and egg; beat on medium speed until smooth, 1 minute. Add the molasses, vanilla, and zest and continue beating until well combined, about 2 minutes. Gradually add the flour mixture; when dough becomes too thick for the mixer, continue beating with a wooden spoon until smooth, about 3 minutes total.

   To make prune puree, place 1/3 cup dried pitted prunes (about 6) and 2 Tbsp water in a food processor; pulse several times until finely chopped. Makes about 1/4 cup.

3. Divide the dough into 3 sections; roll each between 2 sheets of plastic wrap to 1/4-inch thickness. Transfer each dough sheet to a baking sheet, with the plastic wrap still attached, stacking them in three layers. Freeze the dough with the baking sheet, at least 1 hour and up to 2 days.

4. Preheat the oven to 375°F. Spray 2 baking sheets with nonstick cooking spray.

5. Peel off one of the sheets of plastic wrap from a rolled portion of the dough, set the wrap back in place, and remove the wrap on the other side. Lay the dough, loosened sheet down, on a work surface. Cut the dough with a 3-inch gingerbread man cutter. Place the cookies on the prepared baking sheet, 2 inches apart, and bake until just barely dark, about 7–10 minutes. Repeat with the remaining dough. Cool on a rack.

6. To make the icing, in a small bowl, combine the sugar, 2 Tbsp of the hot water, and the vanilla, orange, or lemon extract; stir until smooth. If the icing is too thick, add a few more drops of water. Color with food coloring, if desired. When the cookies are completely cool, decorate with icing.

Coconut Macaroons

Preparation time: 15 minutes
Cooking time: 20 minutes
Serves: 12   Serving size: 2 macaroons

Lighter than air but full of coconut essence, these morsels have that delightful crispy-yet-chewy texture that makes macaroons such a favorite. Yet they contain less than half the coconut of traditional macaroons. The secret: toasting the coconut first, to enhance its flavor, and diluting it with fat-free crisped rice cereal. Keep the macaroons in an airtight container for 1 week; they're even better one day after they're made.

1 1/4	cups sweetened flaked coconut
1 1/2	cups crisped rice cereal
2	egg whites
3	Tbsp granulated sugar
1	tsp vanilla extract
1/8	tsp coconut extract

1. Preheat the oven to 300°F. Line 2 baking sheets with parchment paper or spray with nonstick cooking spray.

2. In a medium baking pan or shallow baking dish, evenly spread the coconut in a thin layer. Bake, stirring every 5 minutes, until lightly browned throughout, about 15 minutes. Remove and let cool. Raise the oven heat to 350°F.

3. In a medium bowl, combine the cooled coconut, rice cereal, egg whites, sugar, vanilla, and coconut extract; stir with a spatula until well combined. Moisten your hands and shape the mixture into walnut-size balls, compacting the balls so that they hold together. Place on the prepared baking sheets. Bake until lightly browned, about 20 minutes; cool at least 30 minutes on a rack before serving.

Exchanges
1/2 Carbohydrate
1/2 Fat

Calories 63
  Calories from Fat . . 23
Total Fat . . . . 3 g
  Saturated Fat . . . . . . 3 g
Cholesterol . . . . 0 mg
Sodium . . . . 65 mg
Carbohydrate . . . . . . 10 g
  Dietary Fiber . . . . . . 0 g
  Sugars . . . . 8 g
Protein . . . . 1 g

Ginger Cookies

Preparation time: 8 minutes
Chilling time: 30 minutes
Cooking time: 7–10 minutes
Serves: 8   Serving size: 2 cookies

There is nothing like the smell of ginger cookies baking in the oven. This one is a soft version that tastes as good as it smells. It is made with half the usual amount of sugar so it won't "snap" when you break it in half, but it will melt in your mouth.

2	cups all-purpose flour
1 1/2	tsp baking soda
1	tsp ground ginger
1	tsp ground cloves
1	tsp cinnamon
1/2	cup stick margarine, softened
1/4	cup firmly packed light brown sugar
1/4	cup granulated sugar
1	egg
2	Tbsp molasses
4	tsp granulated sugar (for dipping)

Exchanges
3 Carbohydrate
1 1/2 Fat

Calories 296
　Calories from Fat . 112
Total Fat . . . . 12 g
　Saturated Fat . . . . . . 2 g
Cholesterol . . . . 27 mg
Sodium . . . . 382 mg
Carbohydrate . . . . . . 42 g
　Dietary Fiber . . . . . . 1 g
　Sugars . . . . 18 g
Protein . . . . 4 g

1. In a medium bowl, whisk the flour, baking soda, ginger, cloves, and cinnamon. Set aside.

2. In a large bowl, with an electric mixer, beat the margarine until smooth. Add the sugars, egg, and molasses. Beat until smooth, about 1 minute. Add the flour mixture to the margarine mixture in thirds, and blend until smooth, 2 minutes. The mixture will be stiff.

3. Refrigerate the dough until thoroughly chilled, at least 30 minutes and up to 1 day.

4. When you're ready to bake, preheat the oven to 350°F. Line a baking sheet with parchment paper. Measure the sugar onto a small plate.

5. Roll the dough into 1-inch balls; place the balls 2 inches apart on the prepared baking sheet.

6. Dip the bottom of a small juice glass into the sugar and flatten the balls gently to about 1/4-inch thickness, dipping the glass into the sugar before flattening each cookie (only a little sugar is needed). Bake until firm, about 7–10 minutes. With a spatula, gently remove the cookies; cool thoroughly on a rack.

Lemon Squares

Preparation time: 20 minutes
Cooking time: 22 minutes
Serves: 16   Serving size: 1 square

Everyone's favorite on the cookie tray, lemon squares are traditionally made with egg- and sugar-rich lemon custard on top of a buttery shortbread crust. This version preserves the tangy lemon flavor and crumbly crust, while sparing you most of the butter and a lot of the sugar. Be sure to use fresh lemon juice and zest—nothing else does quite as well.

1 cup cake flour
2 Tbsp granulated sugar
1 tsp grated lemon zest
1 Tbsp unsalted butter
2 Tbsp canola oil
3 Tbsp low-fat (1%) buttermilk
3 Tbsp all-purpose flour
1/2 tsp baking powder
1/8 tsp salt
2 eggs
2/3 cup granulated sugar
1/3 cup fresh lemon juice

Exchanges

1 Carbohydrate
1/2 Fat

Calories 106
  Calories from Fat . . 29
Total Fat . . . . 3 g
  Saturated Fat . . . . . . 1 g
Cholesterol . . . . 29 mg
Sodium . . . . 42 mg
Carbohydrate . . . . . . 18 g
  Dietary Fiber . . . . . . 0 g
  Sugars . . . . 10 g
Protein . . . . 2 g

1. Preheat the oven to 350°F. Spray an 8 × 8-inch baking pan with nonstick cooking spray.

2. In a small bowl, toss together the cake flour, sugar, and zest. With a pastry blender or 2 knives, cut the butter into the flour mixture until crumbly. Gradually add the oil, stirring with a fork until well blended. Sprinkle with the buttermilk and stir just until the dough begins to hold together.

3. Press the dough into the bottom of the prepared baking pan. Bake until light golden along the edges, 13–15 minutes.

4. In a small bowl, whisk together the flour, baking powder, and salt; set aside.

5. In a large bowl, beat the eggs with the sugar and lemon juice until frothy. Add the reserved flour mixture and beat just until smooth, about 30 seconds. Pour the mixture over the hot crust and bake until the top is set and the edges are lightly browned, about 15 minutes. Cool completely in the pan and cut into 16 squares.

Oatmeal-Raisin Cookies

Preparation time: 15 minutes
Cooking time: 7–9 minutes
Serves: 20   Serving size: 2 cookies

These oatmeal-raisin cookies are packed with flavor and have only 2 grams of fat per cookie. They'll keep in an airtight container up to 1 week or in the freezer for up to 1 month.

1	cup all-purpose flour
1/2	tsp baking powder
1/2	tsp baking soda
3/4	tsp cinnamon
1/4	tsp salt
5	Tbsp stick margarine
1/4	cup granulated sugar
1/4	cup firmly packed light brown sugar
1	egg
1/4	cup low-fat (1%) milk
1	tsp vanilla extract
2 1/4	cups quick-cooking oats
1/3	cup seedless raisins

1. Preheat the oven to 375°F. Line a baking sheet with parchment paper or spray with nonstick cooking spray.

2. In a small bowl, whisk together the flour, baking powder, baking soda, cinnamon, and salt. Set aside.

3. In a medium bowl, with an electric mixer on medium speed, beat the margarine until creamy, 2 minutes. Gradually blend in the sugars. Add the egg and continue beating until smooth, 1 minute. Beat in the milk and vanilla until smooth. Add the flour mixture to the margarine mixture in thirds, and blend until smooth, 2 minutes. Stir in the oats and raisins.

4. Drop the dough by teaspoonfuls onto the prepared baking sheet. Bake until lightly browned, about 7–9 minutes. With a spatula, remove the cookies to a rack and cool completely.

Exchanges
1 Carbohydrate
1 Fat

Calories 115
 Calories from Fat . . 34
Total Fat . . . . 4 g
 Saturated Fat . . . . . . 1 g
Cholesterol . . . . 11 mg
Sodium . . . . 109 mg
Carbohydrate . . . . . . 18 g
 Dietary Fiber . . . . . . 1 g
 Sugars . . . . 7 g
Protein . . . . 3 g

Rolled Sugar Cookies

Preparation time: 25 minutes
Chilling time: 2 hours
Cooking time: 8–10 minutes
Serves: 18   Serving size: 2 cookies

Make these tender, crisp-edged cookies a staple in your holiday baking; no one will guess they have half the fat of traditional sugar cookies, and much less sugar. For best results, chill the dough thoroughly and work fast when rolling the cookies.

2 1/4	cups cake flour
1/2	tsp baking powder
1/4	tsp salt
1/4	cup (1/2 stick) unsalted stick margarine or butter, softened
1/2	cup granulated sugar
2	Tbsp firmly packed light brown sugar
1	egg
1	tsp light corn syrup
1 1/2	tsp vanilla extract
1	cup powdered sugar
2–2 1/2	Tbsp hot water
1/8	tsp vanilla, orange, or lemon extract
1–2	drops food coloring (optional)

1. In a medium bowl, whisk together the flour, baking powder, and salt.

2. In a large bowl, with an electric mixer at medium speed, beat the margarine, granulated sugar, and brown sugar together until fluffy, 2 minutes. Beat in the egg, corn syrup, and vanilla until smooth, 1 minute.

3. Add the flour mixture to the margarine mixture in thirds, until the dough becomes smooth and stiff. Divide the dough in half and wrap in plastic wrap. Chill thoroughly, at least 2 hours.

4. Preheat the oven to 325°F. Arrange the oven racks to divide the oven into thirds. Spray 2 baking sheets with nonstick cooking spray.

Exchanges
2 Carbohydrate

Calories	142
Calories from Fat	. . 27
Total Fat	3 g
Saturated Fat	. . . . . . 1 g
Cholesterol	12 mg
Sodium	47 mg
Carbohydrate	27 g
Dietary Fiber	. . . . . . 0 g
Sugars	14 g
Protein	2 g

5. Working with one piece at a time (and keeping the remaining piece in the refrigerator), roll the dough between 2 sheets of plastic wrap to 1/8-inch thickness. Cut into shapes with a 2-inch cookie cutter and place on the prepared baking sheet. Reroll and reuse the dough scraps. Repeat with the remaining dough.

6. Bake until barely golden along the edges, 8–10 minutes, rotating the baking sheets halfway through to ensure even baking. Let cool 1 minute, then transfer the cookies to a rack.

7. To make the icing, in a small bowl, combine the powdered sugar, 2 Tbsp of the hot water, and the vanilla, orange, or lemon extract; stir until smooth. If the icing is too thick, add a few more drops of water. Color with food coloring, if desired. When the cookies are completely cool, decorate with icing.

Peanut Butter Cookies

Preparation time: 5 minutes
Chilling time: 30 minutes
Cooking time: 7–9 minutes
Serves: 36   Serving size: 1 cookie

This peanut butter cookie is remarkably low in fat but high in flavor and texture. You won't miss the extra sugar and butter. Parchment paper is recommended for even baking and to prevent burning. Buy peanut butter without added sugar for a stronger peanut flavor.

  1 1/4 cups all-purpose flour
      1 tsp baking powder
    1/2 cup stick margarine
    1/2 cup granulated sugar
    1/2 cup creamy (or crunchy) unsweetened peanut butter
      1 egg
      1 tsp vanilla extract
      4 tsp granulated sugar

1. In a small bowl, whisk together the flour and baking powder.

2. In a large bowl, with an electric mixer at medium speed, beat the margarine until smooth. Add the sugar, peanut butter, egg, and vanilla; beat 1 minute. Slowly add the flour mixture and beat just until combined, about 1 minute. The dough will be crumbly. Cover and chill 30 minutes.

3. Preheat the oven to 350°F. Line a baking sheet with parchment paper. Measure the sugar onto a small plate.

4. Roll the dough into 1-inch balls; place the balls 2 inches apart on the prepared baking sheet.

5. Dip the bottom of a small juice glass into the sugar before flattening each ball to about 1/2-inch thickness. Bake until firm, about 7–9 minutes. With a spatula, gently remove the fragile cookies to a wire cooling rack.

Exchanges
1/2 Carbohydrate
1 Fat

Calories 74
  Calories from Fat . . 41
Total Fat . . . . 5 g
  Saturated Fat . . . . . . 1 g
Cholesterol . . . . 6 mg
Sodium . . . . 55 mg
Carbohydrate . . . . 7 g
  Dietary Fiber . . . . . . 0 g
  Sugars . . . . 3 g
Protein . . . . 2 g

Spicy Oat Bars

Preparation time: 8 minutes
Cooking time: 12 minutes
Serves: 9   Serving size: 1 bar

The blend of spices and raisins gives these bars a delectable flavor without a lot of added sugar. Decreasing the sugar can leave cookies less moist, so we've used baking raisins to help make the bars moist and chewy; find them in a box right next to other raisins in the grocery store.

- 1/2 cup all-purpose flour
- 1/2 cup quick-cooking or old-fashioned rolled oats
- 1/2 tsp baking soda
- 1/2 tsp nutmeg
- 1/2 tsp cinnamon
- 1/2 tsp ground allspice
- 1/4 tsp ground cloves
- 1/8 tsp salt
- 1/3 cup firmly packed light brown sugar
- 1/4 cup stick margarine, softened
- 1 egg
- 1 Tbsp low-fat (1%) milk
- 1/3 cup baking raisins

1. Preheat the oven to 350°F. Spray an 8 × 8-inch pan with nonstick cooking spray.

2. In a medium bowl, whisk together the flour, oats, baking soda, nutmeg, cinnamon, allspice, cloves, and salt. Set aside.

3. In a medium bowl, with an electric mixer on medium speed, combine the sugar and margarine. Blend in the egg and milk until smooth. Add the flour mixture to the margarine mixture in thirds, and blend until smooth, 2 minutes. Stir in the raisins.

4. Spread in the baking pan and bake until the edges just start to pull away from the sides of the pan, about 12 minutes. Cool completely and cut into 9 bars.

Exchanges
1 1/2 Carbohydrate
1/2 Fat

Calories 143
  Calories from Fat . . 54
Total Fat . . . . 6 g
  Saturated Fat . . . . . . 1 g
Cholesterol . . . . 24 mg
Sodium . . . . 171 mg
Carbohydrate . . . . . . 20 g
  Dietary Fiber . . . . . . 1 g
  Sugars . . . . 12 g
Protein . . . . 2 g

Rugelach

Preparation time: 25 minutes
Chilling time: 3 hours
Cooking time: 16–18 minutes
Serves: 32   Serving size: 1 piece

Although your Aunt Estelle probably used cream cheese and butter to make her rugelach pastry, our version calls for fat-free cottage cheese and light cream cheese instead. The results would make even Aunt Estelle happy, with drastic fat savings to boot. Store them in an airtight container (they'll keep about 1 week), or freeze them for up to 1 month.

2	cups fat-free cottage cheese
1/2	cup low-fat cream cheese
5	Tbsp granulated sugar
1/4	cup plus 3 Tbsp firmly packed light brown sugar
2	Tbsp canola oil
2	Tbsp unsalted butter or stick margarine, softened
2	tsp vanilla extract
3	cups sifted cake flour
1/2	tsp salt
1	oz walnut halves (about 1/4 cup)
1/4	cup raisins or currants, chopped
1	tsp cinnamon

1. Line a strainer with 2 layers of cheesecloth; add the cottage cheese and, with a spoon, press firmly to squeeze out as much moisture as possible, until the volume reduces to 1 cup.

2. In a large bowl with an electric mixer, combine the pressed cottage cheese, cream cheese, granulated sugar, 3 Tbsp brown sugar, oil, butter, and vanilla; beat on medium speed until fluffy, at least 3 minutes. Stir in the flour and salt until just blended. Wrap in plastic wrap and chill thoroughly, at least 3 hours or overnight.

3. To make the filling, on a small microwavable dish, spread the walnuts in a single layer and cook on high, stirring every minute or so, until slightly darkened and fragrant, 4–5 minutes; set aside. When cool, finely chop.

Exchanges
1 Carbohydrate
1/2 Fat

Calories 105
    Calories from Fat . . 27
Total Fat . . . . 3 g
    Saturated Fat . . . . . . 1 g
Cholesterol . . . . 5 mg
Sodium . . . . 54 mg
Carbohydrate . . . . . . 16 g
    Dietary Fiber . . . . . . 0 g
    Sugars . . . . 6 g
Protein . . . . 3 g

4. In a small bowl, combine the walnuts, 1/4 cup brown sugar, raisins, and cinnamon. Set aside.

5. Preheat the oven to 350°F. Spray 2 baking sheets with nonstick cooking spray.

6. Divide the dough in half. Refrigerate one half, and, on a lightly floured surface, roll the remaining half into a 12-inch circle, neatening the edges. Sprinkle with half of the filling, concentrating the raisins along the outer edges of the circle and pressing slightly so that the filling adheres. Cut the circle like a pizza, creating 16 even triangles. Roll up from the wide end to the point, tucking the point under. Repeat with the remaining dough.

7. Arrange the rugelach 2 inches apart on the prepared baking sheets. Bake, rotating baking sheets halfway through, until lightly browned along the tops, about 16–18 minutes. Cool on a rack.

Classic Cakes

Recipes

Birthday Cake

Preparation time: 20 minutes
Cooking time: 15–18 minutes
Serves: 10   Serving size: 1 piece

This is the snowy-white cake so many of us associate with birthdays, a perfect match for fluffy Seven-Minute Frosting (p. 180). Because it's so delicate and light, it requires careful preparation: make sure the ingredients are room temperature, and that you've measured your ingredients precisely.

    2 cups sifted cake flour
    1 Tbsp baking powder
  1/2 tsp salt
    4 egg whites, room temperature
  2/3 cup granulated sugar, finely ground in a food processor
       or blender for 2 minutes
  1/3 cup canola oil
  1/2 cup buttermilk, room temperature
    2 tsp vanilla extract
    1 tsp almond extract

1. Arrange the oven racks to divide the oven into thirds. Preheat the oven to 350°F. Line 2 8-inch round baking pans with parchment or wax paper rounds and spray with nonstick cooking spray.

2. Sift the flour, baking powder, and salt onto a sheet of wax paper.

3. In a large mixing bowl with an electric mixer on high speed, beat the whites until foamy, 1 minute; gradually add 1/3 cup of the sugar and beat until firm peaks form, 3–4 minutes.

4. In another large mixing bowl with an electric mixer, combine the oil, remaining 1/3 cup sugar, buttermilk, and vanilla and almond extracts; beat until well blended, 30 seconds. Whisk in about half of the flour mixture, then alternately fold in the remaining flour with the beaten whites. Spread evenly in the prepared pans and bake 15–18 minutes, or until a toothpick inserted in the center comes out clean. Cool completely on a rack and frost.

Exchanges
3 Carbohydrate
1 Fat

Calories 270
  Calories from Fat . . 71
Total Fat . . . . 8 g
  Saturated Fat . . . . . . 0 g
Cholesterol . . . . 0 mg
Sodium . . . . 272 mg
Carbohydrate . . . . . . 46 g
  Dietary Fiber . . . . . . 0 g
  Sugars . . . . 24 g
Protein . . . . 5 g

Carrot Cake

Preparation time: 15 minutes
Chilling time: 2 hours
Cooking time: 35–40 minutes
Serves: 12   Serving size: 1 piece

Everyone has a favorite recipe for carrot cake that dates back to the '70s. This new millennium version preserves the cake's famously moist, dense texture without the sugary sweetness. Toasting the nuts brings out their flavor so you can use fewer of them, and the perfect combination of spices compensates for missing fat. It tastes best when refrigerated overnight: make it a day ahead, cover it with plastic wrap, and refrigerate. It will keep up to 4 days.

Cake

- 1/4 cup chopped walnuts
- 1 1/3 cups all-purpose flour
- 1/2 cup granulated sugar
- 1 1/2 tsp baking soda
- 1 tsp baking powder
- 1 tsp cinnamon
- 1/2 tsp ground cloves
- 1/2 tsp ground nutmeg
- 1/2 tsp ground allspice
- 1/4 tsp salt
- 1/4 cup canola oil
- 1/3 cup low-fat (1%) buttermilk
- 2 eggs
- 1 tsp vanilla extract
- 1 1/2 cups grated carrots (about 3 medium)
- 1/2 cup well-drained crushed pineapple

Frosting

- 1 cup powdered sugar, sifted
- 1/4 cup neufchâtel cheese, softened
- 1/4 cup Yogurt Cheese (p. 63) or fat-free brick-style cream cheese

Exchanges
2 Carbohydrate
1 1/2 Fat

Calories 218
  Calories from Fat . . 74
Total Fat . . . . 8 g
  Saturated Fat . . . . . . 1 g
Cholesterol . . . . 39 mg
Sodium . . . . 283 mg
Carbohydrate . . . . . . 33 g
  Dietary Fiber . . . . . . 1 g
  Sugars . . . . 20 g
Protein . . . . 4 g

1. Preheat the oven to 375°F. Spray a 9-inch tube or bundt pan with nonstick cooking spray.

2. In a shallow microwavable dish, spread the walnuts in a single layer and microwave on high, stirring every 30 seconds, until lightly toasted and fragrant, about 2 minutes. Set aside.

3. In a large bowl, whisk together the flour, granulated sugar, baking soda, baking powder, cinnamon, cloves, nutmeg, allspice, and salt. Add the oil, buttermilk, eggs, and vanilla; beat until smooth. Stir in the reserved nuts, the carrots, and the pineapple. Spread evenly in the prepared pan and bake until a toothpick inserted into the center comes out clean, about 35–40 minutes. Cool completely before frosting.

4. To make the frosting, in a medium bowl, stir together the powdered sugar and neufchâtel cheese until smooth. Gently stir in the yogurt cheese, just until blended (do not stir excessively; the frosting will thin). Spread on the cake and refrigerate until chilled, at least 2 hours.

Cheesecake

Preparation time: 15 minutes
Chilling time: 1 day
Cooking time: 40–45 minutes
Serves: 10   Serving size: 1 piece

Adding a little creamy ricotta cheese instead of extra sugar makes all the difference in this recipe. Be sure to puree the cottage and ricotta cheeses until they are absolutely smooth; they give the cake its velvety texture. Make it at least a day ahead of time, to allow the flavors to blend.

1 1/2	cups low-fat (1%) cottage cheese
1/2	cup part-skim ricotta cheese
8	oz neufchâtel cheese, room temperature
3	eggs
1/2	cup sugar
1	Tbsp vanilla extract
2	tsp fresh lemon juice
1/4	tsp salt
4	2 1/2-inch-square reduced-fat graham crackers (1 oz), finely crumbed

1. Position the oven rack in the lower third of the oven. Preheat the oven to 350°F. Line a 9-inch round baking pan with a baking parchment or wax paper round and spray with nonstick cooking spray.

2. In a food processor, puree the cottage and ricotta cheeses until velvety smooth, at least 3 minutes.

3. Add the neufchâtel cheese, eggs, sugar, vanilla, lemon juice, and salt; pulse just until completely smooth, about 30 seconds. Pour into the prepared pan.

4. Pull the oven rack partly out. Place a large roasting pan on the rack; add the filled cheesecake pan. Carefully pour 1/2 inch boiling water into the roasting pan. Bake until the cheesecake is just starting to pull away from the sides of the pan, 40–45 minutes. Cool completely on a rack, then cover with plastic and refrigerate at least 24 hours and up to 2 days.

Exchanges
1 Carbohydrate
1 Lean Meat

Calories 140
  Calories from Fat . . 48
Total Fat . . . . 5 g
  Saturated Fat . . . . . . 3 g
Cholesterol . . . . 77 mg
Sodium . . . . 292 mg
Carbohydrate . . . . . . 15 g
  Dietary Fiber . . . . . . 0 g
  Sugars . . . . 12 g
Protein . . . . 9 g

5. To unmold the cheesecake, cover the pan with tightly stretched plastic wrap, then place a plate on top. Invert the pan and tap gently to release the cake; remove the parchment. Place a cake plate on the cake and invert so that the cake is right-side-up. Press the graham cracker crumbs around the sides of the cake.

Chunky Apple Cake

Preparation time: 12 minutes
Cooking time: 40–45 minutes
Serves: 12   Serving size: 1 piece

This moist cake is attractive, with a deep brown color balanced with the light color of the apple chunks. Make it with your favorite baking apples—we used unpeeled Granny Smiths. Rome, Red Delicious, and Yellow Delicious apples will also taste great.

- 1 cup all-purpose flour
- 1/2 tsp ground nutmeg
- 1/2 tsp cinnamon
- 1/4 tsp salt
- 3/4 cup granulated sugar
- 3 Tbsp stick margarine, softened
- 1 egg
- 2 Tbsp low-fat (1%) milk
- 2 large baking apples, cored and sliced (3 cups)
- 1 tsp granulated sugar
- 1/2 tsp cinnamon

1. Preheat the oven to 350°F. Spray an 8 × 8-inch baking pan with nonstick cooking spray.

2. In a medium bowl, whisk together the flour, nutmeg, cinnamon, and salt.

3. In a medium bowl, with an electric mixer at medium speed, beat the sugar and margarine together until fluffy, 2 minutes. Beat in the egg and milk until smooth, 1 minute. Add the flour mixture to the margarine mixture in thirds, beating until smooth, 2 minutes. With a large spoon, stir in the apples until evenly distributed. Spread the batter in the prepared baking pan.

4. In a small bowl, combine the sugar and cinnamon, then sprinkle evenly on the batter. Bake until browned and the sides start to pull away from the pan, 40–45 minutes.

Exchanges
1 1/2 Carbohydrate
1/2 Fat

Calories 136
    Calories from Fat . . 31
Total Fat . . . . 3 g
    Saturated Fat . . . . . . 1 g
Cholesterol . . . . 18 mg
Sodium . . . . 88 mg
Carbohydrate . . . . . . 25 g
    Dietary Fiber . . . . . . 1 g
    Sugars . . . . 17 g
Protein . . . . 2 g

Martin's Marble Pound Cake

Preparation time: 8 minutes
Cooking time: 25–30 minutes
Serves: 16   Serving size: 1 piece

Maggie's son, Martin, bravely agreed to accept a working version of this cake for his 11th birthday. Here it is, with just a little tweaking. After cooling, sprinkle with just a bit of powdered sugar to offset its golden brown color.

2	cups all-purpose flour
2	tsp baking powder
1/2	tsp baking soda
1/4	tsp salt
1/2	cup stick margarine, softened
1 1/2	cups granulated sugar
3/4	cup egg substitute
1/2	cup evaporated whole milk
1/4	cup unsweetened cocoa powder
1	Tbsp powdered sugar

Exchanges

2 Carbohydrate
1 Fat

Calories 199
  Calories from Fat . . 60
Total Fat . . . . 7 g
  Saturated Fat . . . . . . 1 g
Cholesterol . . . . 2 mg
Sodium . . . . 217 mg
Carbohydrate . . . . . . 32 g
  Dietary Fiber . . . . . . 1 g
  Sugars . . . . 20 g
Protein . . . . 4 g

1. Preheat the oven to 350°F. Spray a 12-cup bundt cake pan with nonstick cooking spray.

2. In a medium bowl, whisk together the flour, baking powder, baking soda, and salt.

3. In another medium bowl, with an electric mixer at medium speed, beat the margarine until creamy, 2 minutes. Gradually blend in the granulated sugar, 1/2 cup at a time. Add the egg substitute and milk, blending until smooth. Add the flour mixture to the margarine mixture in thirds, and blend until smooth, 2 minutes.

4. Put 1 cup of the batter in a small bowl and stir the cocoa into it until evenly colored; set aside. Pour half of the remaining yellow batter in the prepared bundt pan. Spoon the chocolate mixture onto this layer without smoothing it out. Gently spread the rest of the yellow batter on top. To marble, take a knife and cut through the entire batter, swerving the knife back and forth.

5. Bake until golden brown and a toothpick inserted into the center of the cake comes out clean, 30–35 minutes. Cool for 10 minutes, then unmold by sliding a thin knife around the cake, pressing against the pan. Invert onto a cake plate. Cool completely, then sprinkle with powdered sugar.

Orange Chiffon Cake

Preparation time: 20 minutes
Cooking time: 40–45 minutes
Cooling time: 1 1/2 hours
Serves: 14   Serving size: 1 piece

This lighter-than-air cake is breathtaking to look at, and it's full of fresh orange flavor, too. Take the time to warm all the ingredients to room temperature, to finely grind the sugar, and to squeeze fresh orange juice. Every step is critical to making the lightest and most tender cake you've ever tasted.

1 3/4	cups sifted cake flour
3/4	cup granulated sugar, finely ground in a food processor or blender for 2 minutes
1 3/4	tsp baking powder
	Pinch salt
1/2	cup canola oil
3	egg yolks, room temperature
3/4	cup fresh orange juice
3	Tbsp grated orange zest
1	Tbsp vanilla extract
8	egg whites, room temperature
3/4	tsp cream of tartar
1	cup powdered sugar
2	Tbsp fresh orange juice
1	Tbsp orange zest

1. Place the oven rack in the lower third of the oven. Preheat the oven to 325°F.

2. In a large bowl, whisk together the flour, all but 1 Tbsp of the granulated sugar, the baking powder, and salt.

3. In a medium bowl, whisk together the oil, egg yolks, orange juice, zest, and vanilla. Pour into the flour mixture and beat until smooth, 1 minute.

4. In a medium bowl with an electric mixer, beat the egg whites until frothy. Add the cream of tartar and continue beating until soft peaks form. Sprinkle in the remaining granulated sugar and continue beating until stiff peaks form.

Exchanges
2 1/2 Carbohydrate
1 Fat

Calories 238
  Calories from Fat . . 84
Total Fat . . . . 9 g
  Saturated Fat . . . . . . 0 g
Cholesterol . . . . 46 mg
Sodium . . . . 84 mg
Carbohydrate . . . . . . 35 g
  Dietary Fiber . . . . . . 0 g
  Sugars . . . . 20 g
Protein . . . . 4 g

5. With a wire whisk, gently fold the egg whites into the batter just until evenly blended, 30 seconds. Pour into an ungreased 10-inch tube pan with a removable bottom and bake until the cake springs back when lightly pressed in the center, about 40–45 minutes. Let cool upside down for at least 1 1/2 hours, setting the tube over a soda or wine bottleneck.

6. To make the glaze, combine the powdered sugar, orange juice, and zest in a small bowl; blend until smooth. The glaze should be runny enough to drip over the sides of the cake; if necessary, thin with a few drops of water.

7. To unmold the cake, slide a thin knife around the cake, pressing against the pan. Do the same for the tube. Pull the tube upward, to lift the cake from the pan, and slide the knife under the cake to detach it from the bottom. Place on a serving platter and drizzle with the glaze.

Pineapple Upside-Down Cake

Preparation time: 12 minutes
Cooking time: 25–35 minutes
Serves: 12   Serving size: 1 piece

This delicious and pretty dessert uses only 1/4 the usual amount of sugar. A 2-inch square goes a long way. Serve warm with light whipped topping.

2	Tbsp stick margarine
2	Tbsp firmly packed brown sugar
4	slices water-packed canned pineapple, drained
2	maraschino cherries, cut in half
1 1/4	cups all-purpose flour
1 1/2	tsp baking powder
1/2	tsp salt
5	Tbsp stick margarine, softened
1/4	cup granulated sugar
1	egg
1	tsp vanilla extract
1/2	cup low-fat (1%) milk

Exchanges

1 Carbohydrate
1 1/2 Fat

Calories 148
  Calories from Fat . . 66
Total Fat . . . . 7 g
  Saturated Fat . . . . . . 1 g
Cholesterol . . . . 18 mg
Sodium . . . . 231 mg
Carbohydrate . . . . . . 18 g
  Dietary Fiber . . . . . . 0 g
  Sugars . . . . 8 g
Protein . . . . 2 g

1. Preheat the oven to 350°F.

2. In an 8 × 8-inch baking pan, over low heat, melt the margarine. Remove from the heat and stir in the brown sugar. Place the pineapple slices on the sugar mixture, centering the slices closely in the center of the pan so all the pieces are touching. Place a cherry half in the center of each pineapple slice.

3. In a medium bowl, whisk together the flour, baking powder, and salt.

4. In another medium bowl, with an electric mixer at medium speed, beat the margarine and granulated sugar until blended, about 1 minute. Add the egg and vanilla and continue beating until smooth, about 30 seconds. The batter will be thin. Add the flour mixture to the batter in thirds, alternating with milk, blending until smooth, 2 minutes. Spoon the batter on top of the pineapple mixture and spread evenly.

5. Bake until golden brown, about 25–35 minutes. Unmold by sliding a thin knife around the cake, pressing against the pan. Invert onto a cake plate. Serve warm.

Pound Cake

Preparation time: 20 minutes
Cooking time: 45–55 minutes
Serves: 10   Serving size: 1 piece

This pound cake gets a little help from baby food pureed pears. It's best enjoyed a day after it's made, when the complex flavors have melded. Be sure to have all ingredients at room temperature before starting.

1 1/2	cups sifted white flour
1/2	tsp baking powder
1/4	tsp baking soda
1/4	tsp salt
1	egg
2	egg whites
1/2	cup low-fat (1%) buttermilk
1/4	cup pureed pears (find in the baby food aisle)
1 1/2	tsp vanilla extract
1/4	cup unsalted butter or stick margarine, softened
1/2	cup granulated sugar

1. Position the oven rack in the lower third of the oven. Preheat the oven to 325°F. Spray an 8 × 5-inch loaf pan with nonstick cooking spray.

2. Sift the flour, baking powder, baking soda, and salt together and set aside. In a small bowl, whisk the egg and egg whites. In another small bowl, whisk together the buttermilk, pears, and vanilla.

3. In a medium bowl with an electric mixer at medium-high speed, beat the butter until creamy, 30 seconds. Gradually add the sugar and continue beating for 3 minutes. Slowly add the eggs, beating 2 minutes more. Keeping the beating constant, alternate adding the flour mixture in thirds and the buttermilk mixture in halves, ending with the flour mixture, beating just until well combined. Pour into the prepared pan and bake until golden brown, about 45–55 minutes. Cool 10 minutes, then cool completely on a rack.

Exchanges

1 1/2 Carbohydrate
1 Fat

Calories 164	
Calories from Fat . . 48	
Total Fat . . . . 5 g	
Saturated Fat . . . . . . 3 g	
Cholesterol . . . . 34 mg	
Sodium . . . . 139 mg	
Carbohydrate . . . . . . 25 g	
Dietary Fiber . . . . . . 1 g	
Sugars . . . . 11 g	
Protein . . . . 4 g	

Seven-Minute Frosting

Preparation time: 10 minutes
Cooking time: 7 minutes
Serves: 10   Serving size: generous 1/4 cup

This is the marshmallowy, billowy cloud of frosting that makes any cake look ethereal, but it's best on cakes with a light crumb, such as Birthday Cake (p. 169) or Sponge Cake (p. 181). The recipe makes 3 cups, enough to generously frost a two-layer cake. Cakes frosted with Seven-Minute Frosting are best the day they're made, but leftovers can be stored in an airtight cake container up to 2 days in the refrigerator.

> 2 egg whites
> 5 Tbsp water
> 1/2 cup granulated sugar
> 1 tsp light corn syrup
> 1/4 tsp cream of tartar
> 1 tsp vanilla extract

1. Combine the egg whites, water, sugar, corn syrup, and cream of tartar in the top half of a double boiler. Set over simmering water and immediately begin beating with an electric mixer on high speed for 7 minutes.

2. Remove from the heat, add the vanilla, and continue beating until the whites are satiny, with firm peaks, about 1 minute. Use immediately.

Exchanges
1/2 Carbohydrate

Calories 42
 Calories from Fat . . . 0
Total Fat . . . . 0 g
 Saturated Fat . . . . . . 0 g
Cholesterol . . . . 0 mg
Sodium . . . . 12 mg
Carbohydrate . . . . . . 10 g
 Dietary Fiber . . . . . . 0 g
 Sugars . . . . 10 g
Protein . . . . 0 g

Sponge Cake

Preparation time: 30 minutes
Cooking time: 12–15 minutes
Serves: 10   Serving size: 1 piece

This all-purpose, light cake has a wonderful flavor and crumb. Use a 9-inch springform pan and bake for about 20 minutes when preparing Boston Cream Pie (p. 192). For a lemony variation, substitute 1/4 tsp lemon extract and 1 Tbsp grated lemon zest for the almond extract.

1 1/2	Tbsp unsalted butter
1	Tbsp canola oil
1 1/2	tsp vanilla extract
	Few drops almond extract
1	cup sifted cake flour
1/2	cup granulated sugar, finely ground in a food processor or blender for 2 minutes
	Pinch salt
4	eggs

Exchanges

1 1/2 Carbohydrate
1/2 Fat

Calories 144
  Calories from Fat . . 47
Total Fat . . . . 5 g
  Saturated Fat . . . . . . 2 g
Cholesterol . . . . 90 mg
Sodium . . . . 26 mg
Carbohydrate . . . . . . 21 g
  Dietary Fiber . . . . . . 0 g
  Sugars . . . . 10 g
Protein . . . . 4 g

1. Preheat the oven to 375°F. Line 2 9-inch round baking pans with baking parchment or wax paper rounds, spray with nonstick cooking spray, and dust with flour. (You can also use a 9-inch springform pan for a single-layer, high-rising cake.)

2. In a small saucepan over low heat, melt the butter and continue cooking, stirring gently, until golden brown and fragrant, 3–4 minutes (do not allow to burn). Add the canola oil and extracts; set aside and keep warm.

3. Sift the flour twice with 1 Tbsp of the sugar and the salt onto a piece of wax paper. Return to the sifter and set aside.

4. In a large bowl with the electric mixer on high speed, beat the eggs and remaining sugar until the mixture triples in bulk and resembles softly whipped cream, about 10–15 minutes. (The mixture should form ribbons that hold their shape when you lift the beaters and allow the batter to drip.)

5. Sift a third of the flour mixture over the batter, and fold it in gently with a spatula. Repeat two more times. Scoop about 1 cupful of the batter into the saucepan with the melted butter and oil; fold lightly to blend. Then fold it back into the egg mixture until evenly combined. Turn into the prepared pans and bake until a toothpick inserted into the center comes out clean, 12–15 minutes (about 20 minutes for the springform pan). Remove from the pans and cool on a rack.

Classic Cakes   **181**

Strawberry Shortcake

Preparation time: 10 minutes (plus biscuit preparation and baking time)

Cooking time: none

Serves: 8   Serving size: 1 biscuit plus 1/2 cup strawberries

Don't bother making this delight with out-of-season, flavorless, or frozen berries. This dessert should celebrate fresh, at-their-peak berries only! For a different twist, try fresh raspberries or blackberries—or use cut-up peaches or nectarines instead.

> 6 cups hulled fresh strawberries
>
> 2 Tbsp granulated sugar
>
> 1 recipe Buttermilk Biscuits (p. 134), prepared, preferably still hot
>
> 1 cup lite whipped topping

1. In a medium bowl, crush 1 1/2 cups of the strawberries with a fork or potato masher. Slice the remaining whole berries into quarters and add to the crushed berries. Gently stir in the sugar and set aside for 10 minutes.

2. Place a biscuit on each of 8 serving plates; split with a fork and top each with 1/2 cup of the strawberry mixture. Garnish each with 2 Tbsp of whipped topping.

Exchanges

2 Carbohydrate
1 Fat

Calories 197
   Calories from Fat . . 55
Total Fat . . . . 6 g
   Saturated Fat . . . . . . 4 g
Cholesterol . . . . 12 mg
Sodium . . . . 217 mg
Carbohydrate . . . . . . 32 g
   Dietary Fiber . . . . . . 3 g
   Sugars . . . . 11 g
Protein . . . . 4 g

Pies, Crumbles, & Cobblers

Recipes

Buttery Pie Crust

Preparation time: 15 minutes
Cooking time: none
Serves: 8   Serving size: 1/8 recipe

This deliciously tender, buttery crust calls for white (bleached) all-purpose flour; it absorbs less water than unbleached flour, so the crust will be more tender. The extra buttery flavor comes from browning the butter. You can easily make this crust ahead of time and refrigerate or freeze it for later use.

1	Tbsp unsalted butter
1 1/4	cups white all-purpose flour
1/4	tsp salt
	Pinch cinnamon
1/4	cup canola oil
1–2	Tbsp apple juice or cider

1. In a small saucepan over low heat, melt the butter and continue cooking, stirring gently, until golden brown and fragrant, 3–4 minutes (do not allow to burn). Let cool slightly.

2. In a medium bowl, whisk together the flour, salt, and cinnamon.

3. In a small bowl or measuring cup, combine the melted butter with the oil; with a fork, gently stir into the flour mixture until evenly combined. Add the apple juice, 1 Tbsp at a time, just until the dough begins to hold together. Gather the dough into a ball and flatten to a disk.

4. Roll out the dough between 2 sheets of plastic wrap to form a 13-inch circle. Transfer to an 8-inch pie plate, pressing to form a rim; flute the rim, if desired. Use as directed in recipes. (The unbaked crust can be wrapped in plastic and refrigerated for up to 2 days, or frozen up to 1 month.)

Exchanges
1 Starch
1 1/2 Fat

Calories 148
Calories from Fat . . 78
Total Fat . . . . 9 g
Saturated Fat . . . . . . 1 g
Cholesterol . . . . 4 mg
Sodium . . . . 73 mg
Carbohydrate . . . . . . 15 g
Dietary Fiber . . . . . . 0 g
Sugars . . . . 1 g
Protein . . . . 2 g

Graham Cracker Crumb Crust

Preparation time: 15 minutes
Cooking time: 10 minutes
Serves: 8   Serving size: 1/8 recipe

This crumb crust has a wonderful flavor and, after prebaking, a delightful crispness that holds up to creamy fillings. Just a touch of butter adds a lot of flavor, but you can use all oil if you prefer.

- 20 2 1/2-inch-square reduced-fat graham crackers
- 1 egg white, slightly beaten
- 1 Tbsp unsalted butter or stick margarine, melted
- 1 Tbsp canola oil
- 1/4 tsp cinnamon

1. Spray an 8-inch pie plate with nonstick cooking spray. If prebaking the crust, preheat the oven to 350°F.

2. In a food processor or blender, finely crumble the crackers; you should have about 1 1/4 cups. Add the egg white, butter, oil, and cinnamon; pulse until evenly moistened. With a cup or glass, firmly press the crumb mixture into the pie plate (do not cover the lip of the pan with crumbs).

3. If you'll be using the crust with an unbaked pie filling, bake the shell for 10 minutes in the preheated oven. Cool completely before filling.

4. If the crust will be baked after filling it, cover the crust with plastic and chill until firm, about 1 hour. Proceed as the recipe directs.

Exchanges
1 Starch
1/2 Fat

Calories 97
  Calories from Fat . . 36
Total Fat . . . . 4 g
  Saturated Fat . . . . . . 1 g
Cholesterol . . . . 4 mg
Sodium . . . . 124 mg
Carbohydrate . . . . . . 14 g
  Dietary Fiber . . . . . . 0 g
  Sugars . . . . 5 g
Protein . . . . 2 g

Banana Cream Pie

Preparation time: 25 minutes
Cooking time: 14 minutes
Chilling time: 2 hours
Serves: 8   Serving size: 1 piece

The success of this wonderfully creamy pie depends on great bananas. Make sure yours are perfectly ripe and sweet, with plenty of brown "sugar spots." For a delicious, tropical variation, stir a few drops of coconut extract into the custard when you add the vanilla.

3/4	tsp unflavored gelatin
2	Tbsp water
1/3	cup granulated sugar
2	Tbsp cornstarch
1/8	tsp salt
1	cup low-fat (1%) milk
1/2	cup evaporated fat-free milk
2	egg yolks
2	tsp vanilla extract
2	small ripe bananas, thinly sliced
1	Tbsp fresh lime or lemon juice
1	Graham Cracker Crumb Crust (p. 186), prebaked
1/2	cup frozen lite whipped topping

Exchanges

2 Carbohydrate
1 Fat

Calories 203
 Calories from Fat . . 56
Total Fat . . . . 6 g
 Saturated Fat . . . . . . 2 g
Cholesterol . . . . 58 mg
Sodium . . . . 198 mg
Carbohydrate . . . . . . 32 g
 Dietary Fiber . . . . . . 1 g
 Sugars . . . . 19 g
Protein . . . . 5 g

1. In a small saucepan, sprinkle the gelatin over the water; let stand 1 minute until softened, then warm over medium heat, stirring constantly, until melted, 2 minutes. Set aside.

2. In a medium saucepan, whisk together the sugar, cornstarch, and salt. Add the milks and the yolks; whisk until smooth. Cook over medium heat, stirring frequently, until the mixture begins to bubble, 8–10 minutes. Continue cooking, stirring constantly, 1 minute more. Remove from the heat and stir in the dissolved gelatin and the vanilla. Set aside.

3. In a small bowl, toss the bananas with the lime juice.

4. Spread 1/3 of the custard into the pie shell. Top evenly with the sliced bananas, then spread the remaining custard evenly over. Let cool to room temperature, then refrigerate until firm, about 2 hours.

5. Serve each slice with 1 Tbsp of whipped topping, or, for a pretty touch, pipe the whipped topping all along the sides of the pie using a piping bag fitted with a large star tip.

Pies, Crumbles, & Cobblers   **187**

Apple Cranberry Cobbler

Preparation time: 20 minutes
Cooking time: 40 minutes
Serves: 9   Serving size: 1 piece

If you like cranberries, you'll really love them in this cobbler. It is delicious warm or cold, so serve it for breakfast, dessert, or a snack. We kept the skins on the apples we used for added color and texture.

- 3 large baking apples, cored and sliced (6 cups)
- 1 Tbsp fresh lemon juice
- 1 cup fresh whole cranberries or dried cranberries, soaked in water and drained
- 2/3 cup granulated sugar
- 2 Tbsp cornstarch
- 2/3 cup all-purpose flour
- 1 Tbsp granulated sugar
- 1 tsp baking powder
- 1/8 tsp salt
- 1/4 cup stick margarine, cold
- 4 Tbsp low-fat (1%) milk
- 1 egg white
- 1 tsp granulated sugar

1. Preheat the oven to 375°F. Spray an 8 × 8-inch baking pan with nonstick cooking spray.

2. In a medium bowl, combine the apples and lemon juice. Stir in the cranberries, sugar, and cornstarch. Spread in the prepared baking pan.

3. In a medium bowl, whisk the flour, sugar, baking powder, and salt until blended. Cut in the margarine with a pastry blender or 2 knives until the mixture resembles coarse crumbs, 2–3 minutes. Stir in the milk until blended. Lightly flour your hands and form the dough into a ball, then divide into 9 smaller rounds. Flatten each round and place it on the fruit mixture.

Exchanges
2 1/2 Carbohydrate
1 Fat

Calories 200
  Calories from Fat . . 50
Total Fat . . . . 6 g
  Saturated Fat . . . . . . 1 g
Cholesterol . . . . 0 mg
Sodium . . . . 140 mg
Carbohydrate . . . . . . 37 g
  Dietary Fiber . . . . . . 3 g
  Sugars . . . . 26 g
Protein . . . . 2 g

4. With a pastry brush, paint the dough with the egg white, then sprinkle it with the sugar. Bake until the dough turns golden and the fruit begins to bubble, about 40 minutes.

Instead of dough rounds, you may want to make a lattice pattern on the top of the cobbler. To do so, after forming the dough into a ball in step 3, lightly flour a work surface. Roll the dough into a 10-inch round and trim the round to make an 8-inch square. Cut into 8 strips, each about 1/2 inch wide. Place 4 of the dough strips 1/2 inch apart on top of the pie, then arrange the remaining strips over these in a crisscross pattern. You could also flatten the dough and cut out seasonal shapes with cookie cutters or circles with a glass rim.

Apple Pie

Preparation time: 45 minutes
Cooking time: 20–22 minutes
Serves: 8   Serving: 1 piece

This wonderfully flavored pie doesn't need a top crust (and all that extra fat). Instead, it's topped with a crunchy streusel and prettily shaped cutouts made from the dough scraps left over from the bottom crust (try leaf, star, diamond, or crescent shapes). The filling gets its sweetness and thickening from the apples alone, so be picky about which ones you use. Include some that will hold their shape when cooked, and some that will fall apart and give body to the filling.

Streusel/Crust
- 1 Tbsp quick rolled oats
- 1 Tbsp firmly packed dark brown sugar
- 1 Tbsp all-purpose flour
- 1/8 tsp cinnamon
- 1 tsp canola oil
- 1 Buttery Pie Crust (p. 185), prepared but not prebaked (reserve the leftover dough scraps)

Filling
- 1 Tbsp unsalted butter or margarine
- 3 large firm-cooking apples, such as Rome, Braeburn, or Granny Smith, peeled, cored, and sliced
- 2 large soft-cooking apples, such as MacIntosh, Haralson, or Cortland, peeled, cored, and sliced
- 1 Tbsp granulated sugar
- 1 tsp vanilla extract
- 1/2 tsp cinnamon
- 1/8 tsp ground allspice

To prepare the streusel and crust:

1. Arrange the oven racks to divide the oven into thirds. Preheat the oven to 375°F. Spray a baking sheet with nonstick cooking spray.

2. In a small bowl, combine the oats, brown sugar, flour, and cinnamon; add the oil and combine with your fingers until evenly moistened. Spread evenly in a small baking dish or pie plate (a separate dish from the pie crust).

Exchanges
2 1/2 Carbohydrate
2 Fat

Calories 251
  Calories from Fat . 100
Total Fat . . . . 11 g
  Saturated Fat . . . . . . 2 g
Cholesterol . . . . 8 mg
Sodium . . . . 74 mg
Carbohydrate . . . . . . 37 g
  Dietary Fiber . . . . . . 3 g
  Sugars . . . . 19 g
Protein . . . . 2 g

3. With a fork, pierce the pie crust in the pan in several places. Cover with foil and fill with pie weights or dried beans.

4. Gather the remaining pie crust dough scraps together into a ball and flatten. Place between 2 sheets of plastic wrap and roll 1/8 inch thick. With a 2-inch cookie cutter, cut the dough into shapes, re-rolling and using the scraps. Place on the prepared baking sheet.

5. Bake the pie crust and streusel dish on the top oven rack and the cutout shapes on the bottom rack until the cutouts are lightly browned and the streusel is golden, about 10 minutes. Remove the cutouts and streusel; cool on a rack. Remove the foil and pie weights from the pie and continue baking until the crust is golden, 7–10 minutes more. Cool on a rack while you prepare the filling.

To prepare the filling:

1. In a large nonstick skillet over low heat, melt the butter and continue cooking, stirring gently, until golden brown and fragrant, 2–3 minutes (do not allow to burn).

2. Raise the heat to medium; add the apples, sugar, vanilla, cinnamon, and allspice. Cover and cook, stirring occasionally, until the apples are softened, about 10 minutes; uncover and continue cooking, stirring as needed, until the softer apples have fallen apart and the juices have thickened, about 5 minutes more.

3. Pour the filling into the warm crust. Sprinkle evenly with the streusel topping and arrange the cutouts on top in an attractive pattern.

Boston Cream Pie

Preparation time: 15 minutes
Chilling time: 7 hours
Cooking time: 18–20 minutes
Serves: 10   Serving size: 1 piece

This old-fashioned dessert is making a comeback, and no wonder. This version is even more delicious than the one your mother used to make. The intense chocolate glaze is refreshingly bittersweet.

1/4 cup granulated sugar
1/4 cup unsweetened Dutch-process cocoa
1/3 cup low-fat (1%) buttermilk
1/2 tsp vanilla extract
1 recipe Sponge Cake, prepared and cooled (p. 181)
1 1-oz pkg sugar-free, fat-free vanilla pudding
1 3/4 cups fat-free (skim) milk

1. Whisk the sugar and cocoa together in a small saucepan. Gradually add the buttermilk, whisking until smooth. Bring to a boil, stirring constantly; reduce heat and continue boiling for 3 minutes, stirring constantly to prevent burning. Remove from the heat and stir in the vanilla. Let cool.

2. Place a piece of plastic wrap directly on the surface of the glaze to prevent a skin from forming. Refrigerate until cold and thickened, at least 6 hours, or up to 5 days.

3. To assemble the cake, prepare the vanilla pudding according to the package directions for pie filling, using fat-free (skim) milk. Set aside to cool.

4. With a serrated knife, carefully slice the sponge cake in half lengthwise. Spread the pudding over the bottom half, then cover with the top half. Evenly spread a layer of glaze across the top, letting it drizzle down the sides. Refrigerate at least 1 hour before serving.

Exchanges
2 Carbohydrate
1/2 Fat

Calories 169
    Calories from Fat . . 42
Total Fat . . . . 5 g
    Saturated Fat . . . . . . 2 g
Cholesterol . . . . 48 mg
Sodium . . . . 159 mg
Carbohydrate . . . . . . 30 g
    Dietary Fiber . . . . . . 1 g
    Sugars . . . . 16 g
Protein . . . . 3 g

Old-Fashioned Apple Crisp

Preparation time: 12 minutes
Cooking time: 30–35 minutes
Serves: 8   Serving size: 1/8 recipe

The aroma helps make this apple crisp extra scrumptious. Bake it as you eat dinner so you can enjoy it hot with a dollop of lite whipped topping. We used the ever-popular Granny Smith apples, but you could try Macouns, Braeburns, or any combination of firm-fleshed cooking apples.

2	large baking apples, peeled, cored, and sliced (4 cups)
1/3	cup old-fashioned rolled oats
1/3	cup firmly packed brown sugar
1/3	cup all-purpose flour
1/2	tsp cinnamon
1/4	tsp nutmeg
1/4	cup margarine
1	cup lite whipped topping

1. Preheat the oven to 375°F. Spray an 8 × 8-inch round cake pan with nonstick cooking spray.

2. Place the apples in the bottom of the prepared pan; they should almost fill the pan.

3. In a medium bowl, stir together the oats, sugar, flour, cinnamon, and nutmeg. Cut in the margarine with a pastry blender or 2 knives until the mixture resembles coarse crumbs, 2–3 minutes. Spoon this mixture on top of the apples. Bake until the top is crispy and lightly browned, 30–35 minutes. Top each serving with 2 Tbsp whipped topping.

Exchanges
1 1/2 Carbohydrate
1 1/2 Fat

Calories 168
  Calories from Fat . . 64
Total Fat . . . . 7 g
  Saturated Fat . . . . . . 2 g
Cholesterol . . . . 0 mg
Sodium . . . . 72 mg
Carbohydrate . . . . . . 25 g
  Dietary Fiber . . . . . . 2 g
  Sugars . . . . 17 g
Protein . . . . 1 g

Key Lime Pie

Preparation time: 15 minutes
Chilling time: 4 hours
Serves: 8   Serving size: 1 piece

To be truly authentic, seek out key limes, the tiny, golden-skinned Florida limes found in better supermarkets in winter. The common Persian lime works just as well and is a lot easier to use, since it's bigger and has fewer seeds. Whatever you do, use only fresh limes—bottled lime juice has an unacceptably tinny off-flavor.

2	pasteurized egg yolks
1/3	cup freshly squeezed lime juice (approximately 3 Persian limes or 9–10 key limes)
1/3	cup granulated sugar
1	12-oz can evaporated fat-free milk
1	Tbsp grated lime zest
1 1/2	tsp unflavored gelatin
1/4	cup cold water
1	Graham Cracker Crumb Crust (p. 186), prebaked
1/2	cup frozen lite whipped topping (optional)

1. Preheat the oven to 325°F.

2. In a medium bowl, whisk the yolks with the lime juice and sugar until smooth; beat in the milk and zest until smooth.

3. In a small saucepan, sprinkle the gelatin over the water; let soften 1 minute. Heat over low heat, stirring as needed, until the gelatin is dissolved, 2–3 minutes. Let cool slightly, then stir into the egg mixture.

4. Cover and chill until thickened to the consistency of egg white, about 1 hour. (If you need a short cut, place the bowl in a larger, ice water-filled bowl and stir it occasionally until thickened.) Pour into the prepared crust and chill thoroughly, at least 3 hours, before slicing.

Exchanges
2 Carbohydrate
1 Fat

Calories 184
   Calories from Fat . . 49
Total Fat . . . . 5 g
   Saturated Fat . . . . . . 1 g
Cholesterol . . . . 57 mg
Sodium . . . . 188 mg
Carbohydrate . . . . . . 28 g
   Dietary Fiber . . . . . . 1 g
   Sugars . . . . 18 g
Protein . . . . 6 g

5. Serve each slice with 1 Tbsp of whipped topping, if desired, or, for a pretty touch, pipe the whipped topping all along the sides of the pie using a piping bag fitted with a large star tip.

If you can't find pasteurized eggs, follow this step devised by food scientist Shirley Corriher that kills dangerous bacteria in 2 fresh egg yolks: after setting oven temperature, place a wide, shallow pan of cold water in the sink. In a small skillet over low heat, using a spatula, stir the yolks with the lime juice and 1 tsp of the sugar, scraping the bottom of the pan constantly. When the yolks just begin to thicken, about 2–3 minutes, remove the pan from the heat and place it in the cold water pan to stop cooking. Continue with step 2, using the remaining sugar.

Lemon Meringue Pie

Preparation time: 25 minutes
Cooking time: 15 minutes
Standing time: 1 hour
Serves: 8   Serving size: 1 piece

Cutting the fat from this tangy favorite was simple, but reducing the sugar was more of a challenge. We succeeded by flavoring the filling with an abundance of lemon zest, which creates lemony flavor without the sourness of the juice. The secret to a weep-free meringue is to make sure the filling is hot before you spread the meringue over it.

Meringue
- 3 egg whites, room temperature
- 3/4 tsp cream of tartar
- 3 Tbsp granulated sugar
- 1 tsp vanilla extract

Filling
- 1 1/2 cups water
- 1/2 cup granulated sugar
- 1/4 cup cornstarch
- 1/4 tsp salt
- 1 egg
- 1 egg white
- 2 Tbsp grated lemon zest
- 1/3 cup fresh lemon juice
- 1 Buttery Pie Crust (p. 185), prebaked

1. In a medium bowl with an electric mixer, beat the egg whites until frothy. Add the cream of tartar and continue beating until soft peaks form, about 3 minutes. Sprinkle in the sugar and continue beating until stiff peaks form, about 1 minute. Beat in the vanilla.

2. Preheat the oven to 350°F.

3. In a medium stainless steel saucepan (do not use one made of aluminum or iron!), combine the water, sugar, cornstarch, and salt; bring to a boil, stirring frequently. Reduce the heat to medium-low and

Exchanges
2 1/2 Carbohydrate
1 1/2 Fat

Calories 248
 Calories from Fat . . 83
Total Fat . . . . 9 g
 Saturated Fat . . . . . . 1 g
Cholesterol . . . . 31 mg
Sodium . . . . 184 mg
Carbohydrate . . . . . . 37 g
 Dietary Fiber . . . . . . 1 g
 Sugars . . . . 18 g
Protein . . . . 5 g

continue cooking, stirring constantly, until thick, 1 minute. Remove from the heat and set aside.

4. In a small bowl, whisk together the egg, egg white, lemon zest, and lemon juice; whisk in about 2 Tbsp of the sugar syrup to warm it, then add the egg mixture back to the remaining syrup and stir until smooth. Place over medium heat and return to a boil; simmer 30 seconds.

5. Pour the hot filling into the prepared crust. With a rubber spatula, immediately distribute the meringue evenly around the edge, then the center of the pie, making sure it attaches to the pie shell to prevent shrinking. Swirl the meringue with the back of a spoon to create attractive peaks. Bake until the meringue is lightly browned, about 15 minutes. Cool on a rack to room temperature before cutting, at least 1 hour. The pie will keep, covered, in the refrigerator for up to 3 days.

Star-Spangled Cherry Pie

Preparation time: 10 minutes
Cooking time: 70 minutes
Serves: 10   Serving size: 1 piece

This cherry pie calls for frozen unsweetened dark sweet cherries that must be kept frozen until you're ready to mix them in. Thawed cherries will make the pie runny and bleed into the crust. Arrowroot powder is used as the thickener. You will find it in with the other spices at your grocery store. Instead of a full top crust, use shaped cookie cutouts (stars or hearts are great!). Don't let the cooking time of this dessert scare you off—hang out the flag and set the table with patriotic colors while it is baking!

1   Buttery Pie Crust (p. 185); reserve leftover dough scraps
1   Tbsp fresh lemon juice
1   Tbsp water
2   Tbsp arrowroot powder
1/2 tsp vanilla extract
2   12-oz bags frozen unsweetened dark sweet cherries
1/3 cup granulated sugar

1. Gather the pie crust dough scraps together into a ball; flatten. Place between 2 sheets of plastic wrap and roll 1/8 inch thick. With a 2-inch cookie cutter, cut the dough into shapes, rerolling and using the scraps. Set aside.

2. Preheat the oven to 400°F.

3. In a small bowl, combine the lemon juice and water. Add the arrowroot powder and stir until well blended. Stir in the vanilla. If the mixture is too thick, add a few drops of water.

4. In a large bowl, combine the frozen cherries and the sugar. Add the arrowroot mixture, stirring to coat the cherries. Pour into the prepared pie crust. Arrange the cutouts on top in an attractive pattern.

Exchanges
2 Carbohydrate
1 1/2 Fat

Calories 201
  Calories from Fat . . 62
Total Fat . . . . 7 g
  Saturated Fat . . . . . . 1 g
Cholesterol . . . . 3 mg
Sodium . . . . 59 mg
Carbohydrate . . . . . . 33 g
  Dietary Fiber . . . . . . 2 g
  Sugars . . . . 16 g
Protein . . . . 2 g

5. Bake 30 minutes; if the crust seems overly brown, cover the edges with foil. Return to the oven 10 minutes more, then slide a baking sheet under the pie, reduce the heat to 350°F, and continue baking until the filling begins to bubble, about 30 minutes more. Cool completely on a rack.

Be careful to use the correct amount of cherries in this recipe. Two 16-oz bags will make the filling too runny, but you could use 1 1/2 16-oz bags if you can't find the 12-oz ones. And if you've never used arrowroot powder before, it has more thickening power than cornstarch and doesn't break down as readily when heated. Arrowroot comes in a much smaller container than cornstarch because it can lose its thickening ability within a few months.

Pumpkin Pie

Preparation time: 10 minutes
Cooking time: 1 hour
Serves: 8   Serving size: 1 piece

The early Pilgrim pumpkin pie was the whole pumpkin, minus the seeds and top, filled with milk, honey, and spices and then baked. Somewhere along the way a pie replaced the actual pumpkin, to the relief of most of us. This winter squash is most familiar to us as canned pumpkin used at Thanksgiving time. Serve this easy-to-make pie chilled with lite whipped topping sprinkled with a little cinnamon.

    1 15-oz can pumpkin puree
  3/4 cup fat-free half-and-half
  1/2 cup granulated sugar
    2 eggs, slightly beaten
  3/4 tsp cinnamon
  1/4 tsp ground cloves
  1/4 tsp ground ginger
  1/8 tsp nutmeg
    1 Buttery Pie Crust (p. 185), or one deep 8-inch prepared
       pie crust

1. Preheat the oven to 425°F.

2. In a medium bowl, with an electric mixer at medium speed, beat the pumpkin, half-and-half, sugar, eggs, cinnamon, cloves, ginger, and nutmeg until well blended, scraping the sides of the bowl, about 1 minute. Pour into the prepared crust and bake 15 minutes. Reduce the temperature to 350°F and bake until the center is firm, about 45 minutes. Serve chilled.

Exchanges
2 Carbohydrate
2 Fat

Calories 246
  Calories from Fat . . 93
Total Fat . . . . 10 g
  Saturated Fat . . . . . . 2 g
Cholesterol . . . . 59 mg
Sodium . . . . 124 mg
Carbohydrate . . . . . . 34 g
  Dietary Fiber . . . . . . 2 g
  Sugars . . . . 16 g
Protein . . . . 5 g

Puddings & Creamy Desserts

Recipes

Bread Pudding

Preparation time: 5 minutes
Cooking time: 45–55 minutes
Standing time: 30 minutes
Serves: 6   Serving size: 1 piece

This classic dessert turns humble ingredients into something grand. Use a good, sturdy peasant-type bread for best results—or experiment with other types of bread, like sourdough or semolina. The pudding will keep in the refrigerator, covered, for up to 2 days.

    4   oz crust-trimmed 2-day-old whole-wheat bread, torn or
        sliced into bite-size pieces
    2   Tbsp raisins, chopped
    1   cup evaporated fat-free milk
    1   cup low-fat (1%) milk
    2   eggs
  1/4   cup firmly packed dark brown sugar
    2   tsp vanilla extract
1 1/2   tsp cinnamon
  1/4   tsp nutmeg
  1/2   tsp grated orange or lemon zest

1. Spray an 8 × 8-inch baking pan with nonstick cooking spray. Arrange the bread pieces evenly in the prepared pan and sprinkle with the raisins.

2. In a medium bowl, beat together the milks, eggs, brown sugar, vanilla, cinnamon, nutmeg, and zest. Pour the mixture over the bread and refrigerate 30 minutes, periodically pressing the bread down with a spatula to help it absorb the liquid.

3. Preheat the oven to 325°F.

4. Pull the oven rack partly out. Place a large roasting pan on the rack; add the filled bread pudding pan. Carefully pour 1/2 inch boiling water into the roasting pan. Bake until the pudding is puffed and golden brown, about 45–55 minutes. Cool on a rack 10 minutes; serve hot, warm, or room temperature.

Exchanges
2 Carbohydrate

Calories 165
   Calories from Fat . . 27
Total Fat . . . . 3 g
   Saturated Fat . . . . . . 1 g
Cholesterol . . . . 73 mg
Sodium . . . . 198 mg
Carbohydrate . . . . . . 27 g
   Dietary Fiber . . . . . . 1 g
   Sugars . . . . 17 g
Protein . . . . 9 g

Noodle Pudding

Preparation time: 20 minutes
Cooking time: 25–35 minutes
Serves: 9   Serving size: 1/9 recipe

Who says that pasta is a main dish? You can have your pasta in a pudding! We've lightened up the traditional Jewish side dish, called Noodle Kugel, by using fat-free cheeses and milk and more spices for extra flavor. Serve warm with a little unsweetened applesauce on top.

    1   cup fat-free ricotta cheese
    1/2 cup fat-free cream cheese
    1/2 cup plain fat-free yogurt
    1/4 cup low-fat (1%) milk
    1/4 cup granulated sugar
    2   eggs, slightly beaten
    1   Tbsp fresh lemon juice
    1   tsp vanilla extract
    1   tsp cinnamon, divided
    1/4 tsp nutmeg
    2   cups cooked egg noodles, warm
    1   Tbsp firmly packed light brown sugar
    1/2 cup unsweetened applesauce

1. Preheat the oven to 350°F. Spray an 8 × 8-inch baking pan with nonstick cooking spray.

2. In a medium bowl, with an electric mixer at medium speed, beat the ricotta, cream cheese, yogurt, and milk until smooth, about 1 minute. Add the sugar and beat just until blended. Add the eggs, lemon juice, vanilla, 1/2 tsp cinnamon, and nutmeg; beat until smooth, about 1 minute. Stir in the noodles until coated. Spread evenly in the prepared pan.

3. In a small bowl, combine the brown sugar and the remaining cinnamon until blended. Sprinkle over the noodles.

4. Bake uncovered until browned, about 25–35 minutes. Let stand 5 minutes before cutting and serve each piece with a scant tablespoon of applesauce.

Exchanges

1 1/2 Carbohydrate
1 Very Lean Meat

Calories 139
  Calories from Fat . . 16
Total Fat . . . . 2 g
  Saturated Fat . . . . . . 0 g
Cholesterol . . . . 70 mg
Sodium . . . . 134 mg
Carbohydrate . . . . . . 21 g
  Dietary Fiber . . . . . . 1 g
  Sugars . . . . 11 g
Protein . . . . 10 g

Rice Pudding

Preparation time: 5 minutes
Cooking time: 25 minutes
Serves: 6   Serving size: 1/2 cup

The key to this fabulously creamy, yet nearly fat-free dessert is arborio rice—a medium-grain rice typically used for risotto. Arborio rice releases its starch as it cooks, creating a creamy consistency. You can find it in better supermarkets and gourmet grocery stores. Like risotto, this dish must be stirred for about 20 minutes, but the results are well worth the effort. For a delicious variation, substitute ground cardamom for the cinnamon and omit the nutmeg.

    3 cups low-fat (1%) milk
    1/2 cup arborio rice
    2 Tbsp raisins, chopped
    3 Tbsp granulated sugar
    1 cinnamon stick, or 1/4 tsp ground cinnamon
    1/8 tsp nutmeg
    1 tsp vanilla extract
      Pinch salt

1. In a heavy, medium saucepan, combine the milk, rice, raisins, sugar, cinnamon, and nutmeg; bring to a boil, stirring frequently. Reduce the heat to low and simmer, stirring constantly, until the rice is tender and the pudding is creamy and beginning to thicken, about 25 minutes. (The texture should be slightly thinner than you'd like; the pudding will thicken as it cools.)

2. Stir in the vanilla and salt; remove and discard the cinnamon stick, if using. Pour the pudding into a serving bowl or 6 dessert cups. Let cool slightly and serve warm or chilled. The pudding will keep, covered, in the refrigerator for up to 5 days.

Exchanges
1 1/2 Carbohydrate
1/2 Fat-Free Milk

Calories 133
  Calories from Fat . . 12
Total Fat . . . . 1 g
  Saturated Fat . . . . . . 1 g
Cholesterol . . . . 5 mg
Sodium . . . . 74 mg
Carbohydrate . . . . . . 25 g
  Dietary Fiber . . . . . . 1 g
  Sugars . . . . 13 g
Protein . . . . 5 g

Tapioca Pudding

Preparation time: 10 minutes
Standing time: 25 minutes
Serves: 6   Serving size: 1/2 cup

If you're a bit old-fashioned or had a favorite relative who made this pudding, you probably have a soft spot for this homey, soothing dessert. It's just as wonderful as you remember, even if it has lost a little of its fat and sugar. Be sure to use quick-cooking tapioca; regular tapioca requires soaking first.

      2 cups low-fat (1%) milk
    3/4 cup evaporated fat-free milk
      1 egg, lightly beaten
    1/4 cup granulated sugar
      3 Tbsp quick-cooking tapioca
    1/4 tsp nutmeg
         Pinch salt
  1 1/2 tsp vanilla extract

1. In a medium saucepan, combine the milks, egg, sugar, tapioca, nutmeg, and salt; let stand 5 minutes to soften the tapioca.

2. Place on the stove and bring to a full boil over medium heat, stirring constantly, 5–8 minutes. Remove from the heat (do not stir longer or the tapioca can become gluey). Stir in the vanilla. Let cool 20 minutes, then pour into a serving bowl or 6 dessert cups. Serve warm or chilled. The pudding will keep, covered, in the refrigerator for up to 5 days.

Exchanges
1 Carbohydrate
1/2 Fat-Free Milk

Calories 119
    Calories from Fat . . 16
Total Fat . . . . 2 g
    Saturated Fat . . . . . . 1 g
Cholesterol . . . . 39 mg
Sodium . . . . 103 mg
Carbohydrate . . . . . . 20 g
    Dietary Fiber . . . . . . 0 g
    Sugars . . . . 14 g
Protein . . . . 6 g

Tiramisù

Preparation time: 15 minutes
Chilling time: 6 hours
Serves: 8   Serving size: 1/8 recipe

This heavenly dessert translates to "pick me up" in Italian—and it lives up to its name. Thanks to the recent availability of pasteurized eggs, it's also a snap to make—no need to heat the eggs for safety's sake. For best results, make sure the bowl and beaters are squeaky clean when you beat the egg whites—even a trace of grease will hinder their ability to fluff up. You can try an 11-oz pound cake sliced into finger-sized strips in this recipe instead of ladyfingers.

2	pasteurized eggs, separated, room temperature
2	pasteurized egg whites, room temperature
2	Tbsp granulated sugar
1	Tbsp Madeira or dry port
1 1/4	cups part-skim ricotta
1/2	cup cooled espresso or extra-strong coffee
15	ladyfinger cookies
2	tsp unsweetened cocoa

1. In a large bowl, with an electric mixer at high speed, beat all 4 egg whites until firm (not stiff) peaks form; set aside.

2. In another large bowl, with an electric mixer at medium speed, beat the 2 egg yolks with the sugar and Madeira until frothy and lemon colored, 1 minute. Gently stir in the ricotta. Fold in the beaten egg whites.

3. Pour the espresso into a shallow bowl or pie plate. One at a time, dip the ladyfingers into the espresso and arrange on the bottom of an 8 × 8-inch glass dish or baking pan (they should fit snugly; break some cookies in half, if necessary, to fit).

4. Spread the egg white mixture evenly over the ladyfingers. Cover and refrigerate 6 hours or up to 12 hours. Just before serving, sprinkle evenly with the cocoa.

Exchanges
1/2 Carbohydrate
1 Medium-Fat Meat

Calories 114
    Calories from Fat . . 44
Total Fat . . . . 5 g
    Saturated Fat . . . . . 2 g
Cholesterol . . . . 89 mg
Sodium . . . . 88 mg
Carbohydrate . . . . . . 10 g
    Dietary Fiber . . . . . . 0 g
    Sugars . . . . 7 g
Protein . . . . 7 g

Trifle

Preparation time: 20 minutes
Chilling time: 4 hours
Serves: 10   Serving size: 1/2 cup

Trifle is a traditional English creation made with ladyfingers or a similar cake soaked in rum or sherry and layered with custard, raspberries, and whipped cream. This recipe leaves out the rum but includes directions for making your own creamy custard. Ladyfinger cookies, sometimes called savoiardi biscuits, can be found in the specialty cookie section of some grocery stores and gourmet grocery stores, or sometimes in the freezer section of your grocery store. Fresh raspberries are the best, but an equal amount of frozen will work too; but don't thaw before using. This dish is best if made ahead 4–8 hours or overnight.

4	Tbsp granulated sugar
1	Tbsp cornstarch
1/8	tsp salt
1 1/3	cups low-fat (1%) milk
1	egg, lightly beaten
3/4	tsp vanilla extract
1 1/2	cups frozen fat-free whipped topping
1	3-oz pkg ladyfinger cookies (about 24), each broken in half
3	cups fresh raspberries (reserve 1/2 cup for topping)

1. In a medium nonstick skillet, whisk the sugar, cornstarch, and salt. Add the milk and stir to blend. Cook over medium heat, stirring constantly, until mixture bubbles and thickens, about 4 minutes. Remove from the heat.

2. In a small bowl, combine the egg with 1/4 cup of the hot mixture; stir to blend. Add back to the skillet and cook over medium heat, stirring constantly, until the mixture begins to bubble, about 3 minutes. Remove from the heat and transfer to a medium bowl; cool 5 minutes. Stir in the vanilla. Fold in 1 cup of the whipped topping until well blended.

3. In a deep 2-qt glass bowl, line the bottom and sides with 8 ladyfingers, breaking some

Exchanges
1 1/2 Carbohydrate

Calories 110
  Calories from Fat . . 15
Total Fat . . . . 2 g
  Saturated Fat . . . . . . 0 g
Cholesterol . . . . 53 mg
Sodium . . . . 69 mg
Carbohydrate . . . . . . 20 g
  Dietary Fiber . . . . . . 3 g
  Sugars . . . . 12 g
Protein . . . . 3 g

if needed to fit. Sprinkle 3/4 cup of the raspberries in the bowl and top with 1/2 of the custard. Repeat another layer of 8 ladyfingers, 3/4 cup raspberries, and the remaining custard. Top with the remaining 8 ladyfingers, 1/2 cup of the whipped topping, and the remaining raspberries.

4. Cover and chill for at least 4–8 hours or overnight.

Try brushing the ladyfinger halves with 2 Tbsp of pineapple juice before assembling the trifle. Some like the rum-type flavor this gives.

Vanilla Ice Cream

Preparation time: 5 minutes
Chilling time: 4 hours
Freezing time: varies with your ice-cream maker
Serves: 8   Serving size: 1/2 cup

This ice cream has a silky-smooth, creamy texture with very little fat, thanks to the smoothness of marshmallow fluff and nonfat sour cream. Since a wonderful vanilla flavor is essential, be sure to use only pure vanilla extract, not imitation—preferably one without corn syrup in the ingredients list. Or, even better, use a real vanilla bean—you'll be amazed at the difference. (If you're using a vanilla bean, simply split the bean in half lengthwise with a small sharp knife, and use the tip of the knife to scrape out the flavorful seeds. You can put the empty bean in your sugar bowl; it will make delicious vanilla-flavored sugar.)

> 4 cups fat-free half-and-half
> 1 cup fat-free sour cream
> 1 Tbsp vanilla extract, or the seeds of 1 plump vanilla bean
> 1 1/2 cups marshmallow fluff

1. In a large bowl, whisk together the half-and-half and sour cream just to blend (don't worry about lumps; they'll disappear in the ice-cream maker) and stir in the vanilla. Cover and refrigerate until thoroughly chilled (40°F), at least 4 hours.

2. Whisk in the marshmallow fluff and freeze in an ice-cream maker following the manufacturer's instructions.

3. The ice cream is best enjoyed within a few hours of making it, but it can be stored in the freezer up to 5 days. Let it soften in the refrigerator 30 minutes before scooping it.

Exchanges
2 Carbohydrate

Calories 166
    Calories from Fat . . 15
Total Fat . . . . 2 g
    Saturated Fat . . . . . . 1 g
Cholesterol . . . . 10 mg
Sodium . . . . 223 mg
Carbohydrate . . . . . . 32 g
    Dietary Fiber . . . . . . 0 g
    Sugars . . . . 20 g
Protein . . . . 4 g

Variations
Chocolate Chip Ice Cream: Coarsely chop 2 oz semi-sweet chocolate chips (or 2 oz bittersweet chocolate) and add to the cooled ice cream mixture just before freezing.

Strawberry Ice Cream: Stir 1 cup frozen sliced strawberries into the ice cream mixture when it is nearly frozen, then continue until the desired texture is reached.

Toasted Coconut Ice Cream: Preheat the toaster oven to 300°F. Spread 1/4 cup sweetened flaked coconut in the toaster oven pan, and bake, stirring occasionally, until lightly browned throughout, about 8 minutes. Let cool completely and add it and 1/4 tsp coconut extract to the other ingredients.

Chocolate Magic

Recipes

Brownies

Preparation time: 15 minutes
Cooking time: 15–20 minutes
Serves: 16   Serving size: 1 brownie

Two different "layers" of chocolate—cocoa plus bittersweet chocolate—make these cake-like, chewy brownies something special. They should seem slightly underbaked when you take them out of the oven; as they cool, they'll become chewy and firm.

2/3	cup all-purpose flour
1/3	cup Dutch-process cocoa
2	tsp instant espresso powder
1/4	tsp baking soda
1/4	tsp salt
2	oz bittersweet chocolate, finely chopped
2	Tbsp canola oil
1/3	cup unsweetened applesauce
1/4	cup firmly packed dark brown sugar
1/4	cup granulated sugar
2	Tbsp dark corn syrup
2	tsp vanilla extract
2	egg whites

Exchanges

1 Carbohydrate
1/2 Fat

Calories 92
    Calories from Fat . . 32
Total Fat . . . . 4 g
    Saturated Fat . . . . . . 1 g
Cholesterol . . . . 0 mg
Sodium . . . . 67 mg
Carbohydrate . . . . . . 16 g
    Dietary Fiber . . . . . . 1 g
    Sugars . . . . 10 g
Protein . . . . 2 g

1. Preheat the oven to 325°F. Spray an 8 × 8-inch baking pan with nonstick cooking spray.

2. In a small bowl, whisk together the flour, cocoa, espresso powder, baking soda, and salt; set aside.

3. In a heavy, medium saucepan, combine the bittersweet chocolate and the oil; cook over low heat, stirring constantly, until the chocolate is completely melted, about 2 minutes. Remove from the heat.

4. Stir in the applesauce, sugars, corn syrup, and vanilla; beat until smooth, about 1 minute. Add the egg whites and continue beating until the sugar is dissolved, 1 minute more. Add the reserved flour mixture and stir gently until smooth, about 2 minutes.

5. Spread evenly in the prepared pan and bake until a toothpick inserted into the center comes out nearly clean, with a few fudgy crumbs, about 15–20 minutes. Cool completely on a rack before cutting.

Chocolate Biscotti

Preparation time: 30 minutes
Cooking time: 80 minutes
Serves: 20   Serving size: 2 biscotti

These are intensely chocolaty, crisp cookies that store beautifully (up to 2 weeks in an airtight container, and up to 3 months in the freezer). Best enjoyed dipped in a cup of hot coffee or peppermint tea.

1/4	cup whole almonds
1 3/4	cups all-purpose flour
1/3	cup unsweetened Dutch-process cocoa powder
1	tsp baking soda
1/4	tsp salt
1	oz bittersweet chocolate, finely chopped
1	Tbsp instant espresso powder
1/2	cup granulated sugar
2	Tbsp unsalted butter or margarine, softened
2	eggs
1	egg white
1	tsp vanilla extract
1	tsp almond extract

1. Adjust the oven racks to divide the oven into thirds. Preheat the oven to 300°F. Line 2 baking sheets with parchment paper.

2. On a small microwavable dish, spread the almonds in a single layer and cook on high, stirring every minute or so, until slightly darkened and fragrant, 4–5 minutes; set aside. When cool, coarsely chop.

3. Sift together the flour, cocoa, baking soda, and salt.

4. In a food processor or blender, combine the chocolate and espresso powder with about 1/2 cup of the flour mixture and pulse 15–20 seconds, until finely crumbed.

5. In a large bowl with an electric mixer, beat the sugar and butter until fluffy, 1 minute, then beat in the eggs, egg white, and the extracts. On low speed, beat in the chocolate mixture and the remaining flour mixture. Stir in the almonds by hand (dough will be thick).

Exchanges
1 Carbohydrate
1/2 Fat

Calories 97
  Calories from Fat . . 31
Total Fat . . . . 3 g
  Saturated Fat . . . . . . 1 g
Cholesterol . . . . 24 mg
Sodium . . . . 102 mg
Carbohydrate . . . . . . 15 g
  Dietary Fiber . . . . . . 1 g
  Sugars . . . . 6 g
Protein . . . . 3 g

6. Sprinkle a work surface with flour. Turn out the dough and divide into two pieces. With floured hands, roll each into a 12-inch log. Place each log diagonally across each prepared baking sheet. Brush off any excess flour.

7. Bake until firm, 40 minutes, switching baking sheets from top to bottom halfway through baking. Let cool 10 minutes, then carefully slice with a serrated knife into 1/2-inch slices. Return the cookies to the baking sheet and continue baking 30 minutes more, again switching baking sheets halfway through. Cool completely on a rack.

Chocolate Cherry Bars

Preparation time: 15 minutes
Cooking time: 15–20 minutes
Serves: 16   Serving size: 1 piece

This recipe is a chocolate lover's dream—it is so rich in chocolate. The cherries add a cheery red color and a delightful blend of flavors. We tried adding applesauce and mixing the ingredients with a mixer, but found this combination of ingredients and simpler cooking method yielded the richest, chewiest bar.

1/2 cup stick margarine
1/2 cup granulated sugar
  1 egg, slightly beaten
1/2 cup cocoa
  1 tsp vanilla extract
1/2 tsp baking powder
1/8 tsp baking soda
1/2 cup all-purpose flour
1/2 cup low-sugar cherry pie filling
  2 Tbsp mini chocolate chips

1. Preheat the oven to 325°F. Spray an 8 × 8-inch baking pan with nonstick cooking spray.

2. In a medium saucepan, melt the margarine. Add the sugar and stir until smooth and slightly cooled, 2 minutes. Blend in the egg. Add the cocoa, vanilla, baking powder, and baking soda; stir until the cocoa is fully incorporated, 1 minute. Add the flour and stir just until smooth, 1 minute.

3. Spread the batter in the prepared baking pan and top evenly with pie filling. Bake until the top becomes slightly crusty, 8–10 minutes, then sprinkle on the chocolate chips. Bake until a toothpick inserted into the center comes out clean with a few moist crumbs, about 8–10 minutes.

Exchanges
1 Carbohydrate
1 Fat

Calories 111
  Calories from Fat . . 62
Total Fat . . . . 7 g
  Saturated Fat . . . . . . 1 g
Cholesterol . . . . 13 mg
Sodium . . . . 93 mg
Carbohydrate . . . . . . 13 g
  Dietary Fiber . . . . . . 1 g
  Sugars . . . . 8 g
Protein . . . . 1 g

Chocolate Chip Cookies

Preparation time: 10 minutes
Cooking time: 14–16 minutes
Serves: 36   Serving size: 1 cookie

We had to include a special recipe for this all-time favorite cookie. Although there are many variations, we found this version to be a hit with crispy, cake-like, and chewy chocolate chip cookie lovers alike.

1 1/2 cups all-purpose flour
1/2 tsp baking soda
1/4 tsp salt
1/2 cup stick margarine
1/2 cup granulated sugar
1/4 cup packed light brown sugar
1 egg
1/4 cup no-sugar-added applesauce
2 Tbsp low-fat (1%) milk
2 tsp vanilla extract
1/2 cup chocolate chips

1. Preheat the oven to 350°F. Spray 2 baking sheets with nonstick cooking spray.

2. In a small bowl, whisk together the flour, baking soda, and salt.

3. In a large bowl, with an electric mixer at medium speed, beat the margarine until fluffy. Add the sugars, egg, applesauce, milk, and vanilla and beat 1 minute. Slowly add the flour mixture and beat until combined, about 1 minute. Stir in the chocolate chips.

4. Drop the dough by teaspoonfuls onto the prepared baking sheet. Bake until lightly browned, 14–16 minutes. Remove and cool on a baking rack.

Exchanges
1/2 Carbohydrate
1/2 Fat

Calories 72
  Calories from Fat . . 31
Total Fat . . . . 3 g
  Saturated Fat . . . . . . 1 g
Cholesterol . . . . 6 mg
Sodium . . . . 66 mg
Carbohydrate . . . . . . 10 g
  Dietary Fiber . . . . . . 0 g
  Sugars . . . . 6 g
Protein . . . . 1 g

Chocolate Doughnuts

Preparation time: 6 minutes
Cooking time: 7–8 minutes per batch
Serves: 24   Serving size: 1 doughnut

Thanks to a nonstick mini-doughnut baking pan, available in kitchen specialty stores, you can prepare old-fashioned doughnuts in your oven instead of the deep-fat fryer—saving oodles of fat.

11/2 cups all-purpose flour
1/3   cup unsweetened Dutch-process cocoa powder
1   tsp baking powder
1/2   tsp salt
2   large eggs
2/3   cup granulated sugar
1   tsp vanilla extract
1/2   cup espresso or strong coffee, cooled
2   Tbsp canola oil

1. Preheat oven to 325°F. Spray 2 mini-doughnut pans with nonstick cooking spray.

2. In a small bowl, whisk together flour, cocoa, baking powder, and salt.

3. In a large bowl, beat eggs, sugar, and vanilla until thick and frothy.

4. Combine the coffee and oil and add to the egg mixture, alternating with the flour mixture. Place about 2 tsp batter into each well of the prepared doughnut pan, filling them about halfway. Bake 7–8 minutes, or until firm and springy to the touch. Let cool on rack 1 minute, then carefully remove doughnuts and cool completely. Repeat with remaining batter.

Exchanges
1 Carbohydrate

Calories 68
   Calories from Fat . . 16
Total Fat . . . . 2 g
   Saturated Fat . . . . . . 0 g
Cholesterol . . . . 18 mg
Sodium . . . . 69 mg
Carbohydrate . . . . . . 12 g
   Dietary Fiber . . . . . . 1 g
   Sugars . . . . 6 g
Protein . . . . 2 g

Chocolate Frosting or Glaze

Preparation time: 10 minutes
Chilling time: 6 hours
Serves: 12   Serving size: 2 Tbsp

This frosting, based on a clever technique by chocolate maven Alice Medrich, is so rich and chocolaty you'll swear it was made with the finest chocolate. In fact, it just contains good-quality cocoa and plenty of it. If you need a fudgy glaze or sauce, simply prepare the recipe with twice the milk.

1	cup confectioners sugar
1/4	cup Dutch-process unsweetened cocoa
2 or 4	Tbsp low-fat (1%) milk (see above)
1/2	cup brick-style light cream cheese, room temperature
1/4	tsp vanilla extract

1. In a 4-cup glass measuring cup or microwavable bowl, whisk together the sugar, cocoa, and milk until a smooth paste forms. (If too thick to stir, don't worry—it will melt as it heats.) Cover with plastic wrap and microwave on high until the mixture begins to bubble, about 3 minutes. Set aside.

2. In a small bowl, gently stir the cream cheese until it is smooth and spreadable. Pour a little of the chocolate mixture over the cream cheese and gently stir it in. Repeat with a little more chocolate at a time, stirring gently after each addition, until all the chocolate is used. (Do not beat—this will cause the frosting to thin.) Stir in the vanilla.

3. Cover and refrigerate until stiff enough to spread, at least 6 hours and preferably overnight.

Exchanges
1 Carbohydrate

Calories 67
   Calories from Fat . . 20
Total Fat . . . . 2 g
   Saturated Fat . . . . . . 1 g
Cholesterol . . . . 7 mg
Sodium . . . . 41 mg
Carbohydrate . . . . . . 11 g
   Dietary Fiber . . . . . . 1 g
   Sugars . . . . 10 g
Protein . . . . 1 g

This frosting may be prepared up to 1 week in advance and stored in the refrigerator.

Chocolate Mousse

Preparation time: 50 minutes
Standing/chilling time: 3 1/2 hours
Serves: 6   Serving size: 1/2 cup

This mousse is so mouth-fillingly chocolaty you'll feel the half-cup serving is more than generous. While pasteurized egg whites are a must to ensure safety, you can also use the equivalent in powdered egg whites, found in most grocery stores in the baking section. Grate your zest carefully, avoiding including any white pith of the orange. For a slightly sweeter taste, you can use semisweet chocolate, but be sure to use a bar rather than waxy-textured morsels. The mousse can be prepared up to 2 days ahead.

3/4	cup low-fat (1%) milk
	Zest of 1/2 small orange
1	tsp unflavored gelatin
2	Tbsp coffee, cooled
1	egg
1/2	cup firmly packed light brown sugar
2/3	cup unsweetened cocoa, preferably Dutch process
2	oz bittersweet chocolate, finely chopped
2	tsp vanilla extract
4	pasteurized egg whites, room temperature
1/2	tsp cream of tartar

1. In a small saucepan over medium heat, warm the milk and orange zest, stirring occasionally, until bubbles appear along the rim of the saucepan, about 1 minute; remove from heat and let steep 10 minutes.

2. In a small bowl, sprinkle the gelatin over the coffee and let stand until softened, 2 minutes.

3. Meanwhile, in a medium saucepan, whisk together the egg, all but 1 Tbsp of the brown sugar, and the cocoa; cook over low heat, whisking constantly, until thickened, about 5 minutes. Remove from the heat and add the softened gelatin mixture, stirring until the gelatin has completely dissolved, about 3 minutes. Add the chocolate and vanilla and stir until the chocolate melts, 1 minute. Set aside to cool to room temperature, about 30 minutes.

Exchanges
2 Carbohydrate
1/2 Fat

Calories 173
  Calories from Fat . . 47
Total Fat . . . . 5 g
  Saturated Fat . . . . . . 2 g
Cholesterol . . . . 37 mg
Sodium . . . . 71 mg
Carbohydrate . . . . . . 31 g
  Dietary Fiber . . . . . . 3 g
  Sugars . . . . 25 g
Protein . . . . 7 g

4. In a large bowl with an electric mixer, beat the egg whites until frothy, 30 seconds; add the cream of tartar and continue beating until soft peaks form, 3–4 minutes. Sprinkle with 1 Tbsp brown sugar and continue beating just until stiff, 1–2 minutes longer.

5. With a rubber spatula, scoop about 1/4 of the egg whites into the chocolate mixture to lighten it, folding in gently. Then fold the chocolate mixture back into the remaining egg whites, folding gently until well blended.

6. Spoon into 6 dessert cups or a 4-cup dessert bowl and chill until set, 2 1/2–3 hours. If storing longer, cover with plastic wrap, being careful not to touch the surface of the mousse with the wrap.

Chocolate Peanut Puffed Rice Bars

Preparation time: 8 minutes
Standing time: 10 minutes
Serves: 9   Serving size: 1 piece

These bars are great in kids' lunchboxes or at a birthday party—and they're so easy to make!

1/4	cup light corn syrup
2	Tbsp creamy peanut butter
2	Tbsp mini-chocolate chips
2	cups puffed rice cereal

1. Spray an 8 × 8-inch baking pan with nonstick cooking spray.

2. In a medium saucepan, combine the corn syrup, peanut butter, and chocolate chips. Cook on low heat until the peanut butter and chocolate chips are melted, 3 minutes. Remove from the heat and stir in the puffed rice until well incorporated. Spread in the prepared pan and cool for 10 minutes before cutting.

Exchanges
1 Carbohydrate

Calories 70
  Calories from Fat . . 23
Total Fat . . . . 3 g
  Saturated Fat . . . . . . 1 g
Cholesterol . . . . 0 mg
Sodium . . . . 28 mg
Carbohydrate . . . . . . 12 g
  Dietary Fiber . . . . . . 0 g
  Sugars . . . . 6 g
Protein . . . . 1 g

Devil's Food Cake

Preparation time: 25 minutes
Cooking time: 25 minutes
Serves: 12   Serving size: 1 piece

This is a truly American creation, so intensely chocolaty a thin slice makes a big impact. It's made possible by American-style cocoa, which is higher in acid than Dutch-process cocoa. The reaction of the cocoa's acid with the baking soda produces that distinctive Devil's Food flavor. In other words, don't use Dutch-process cocoa in this recipe; it won't work!

1 3/4	cups cake flour
1/2	cup American-style unsweetened cocoa
1 1/2	tsp baking powder
1/2	tsp baking soda
1/2	tsp salt
2/3	cup granulated sugar
1/4	cup unsalted butter or margarine, softened
1	egg, room temperature
2	egg whites, room temperature
2	tsp vanilla extract
1	cup low-fat (1%) buttermilk
1	recipe Chocolate Frosting (p. 219)

1. Arrange the oven racks to divide the oven into thirds. Preheat the oven to 350°F. Line 2 8-inch round baking pans with parchment or wax paper rounds and spray with nonstick cooking spray.

2. In a medium bowl, whisk together the flour, cocoa, baking powder, baking soda, and salt until evenly combined; set aside.

3. In a large bowl with an electric mixer, beat the sugar and butter together until fluffy, 1–2 minutes. Add the egg and egg whites, one at a time, beating well after each addition. Beat in the vanilla. Keeping the beating constant, alternate adding the flour mixture in thirds and the buttermilk in halves, ending with the flour mixture, beating just until well combined.

4. Turn into the prepared pans and bake until a toothpick inserted in the center comes out clean, about 25 minutes. Cool completely on a rack and frost with Chocolate Frosting.

Exchanges
2 1/2 Carbohydrate
1 Fat

Calories 239
  Calories from Fat . . 66
Total Fat . . . . 7 g
  Saturated Fat . . . . . . 4 g
Cholesterol . . . . 36 mg
Sodium . . . . 273 mg
Carbohydrate . . . . . . 41 g
  Dietary Fiber . . . . . . 2 g
  Sugars . . . . 22 g
Protein . . . . 6 g

*I*ndex

Alphabetical List of Recipes

Subject Index

Books from the American Diabetes Association

Cooking and Nutrition

Cooking with the Diabetic Chef
Chris Smith

Introducing the first cookbook ever written for people with diabetes by a chef with diabetes! Chris Smith is living proof you can eat the foods you love and live healthy with diabetes. Pizza, chocolate, butter, burritos, sausage, veal roast, stir fry. Imagine sinking your teeth into Chocolate Chip Pancakes, Succulent Steak Teriyaki, Tender melt-in-your-mouth ribs, Dreamy chocolate cake and many more!
One Low Price: $19.95
Order #4630-01

More Diabetic Meals in 30 Minutes—or Less!
Robyn Webb

Robyn Webb is back weaving her magic in your kitchen! She's whipped up hundreds more simply sensational recipes from mouth watering appetizers and succulent seafood dishes to tantalizing desserts. Choose from any of 225 fabulous recipes that not only satisfy your appetite and your cravings but also meet ADA nutritional guidelines. Each recipe gives you nutritional content and exchanges as well as fat and calorie counts.
Nonmember: $16.95
Member: $14.95
Order #4629-01

The Great Chicken Cookbook for People with Diabetes
Beryl M. Marton

Now you can have chicken any way you want it—and healthy too! More than 150 great-tasting, low-fat chicken recipes in all, including baked chicken, braised chicken, chicken casseroles, grilled chicken, rolled and stuffed chicken, chicken soups, chicken stir-fry, chicken with pasta, and many more.
Nonmember: $16.95
Member: $14.95
Order #4627-01

The New Soul Food Cookbook for People with Diabetes
Fabiola Demps Gaines, RD, LD
Roniece Weaver, RD, LD

Dig into sensational low-fat recipes from the first African American cookbook for people with diabetes. More than 150 recipes in all, including Shrimp Jambalaya, Fried Okra, Orange Sweet Potatoes, Corn Muffins, Apple Crisp, and many more.
Nonmember: $14.95
Member: $12.95
Order #4623-01

The Diabetes Snack Munch Nibble Nosh Book
Ruth Glick

Choose from 150 low-sodium, low-fat snacks and mini-meals such as Pizza Puffs, Mustard Pretzels, Apple-Cranberry Turnovers, Bread Puzzle, Cinnamon Biscuits, Pecan Buns, Alphabet Letters, Banana Pops, and many others. Special features include recipes for one or two and snack ideas for hard-to-please kids. Nutrient analyses, preparation times, and exchanges are included with every recipe.

Nonmember: $14.95
Member: $13.95
Order #4622-01

The ADA Guide to Healthy Restaurant Eating
Hope S. Warshaw, MMSc, RD, CDE

Finally! One book with all the facts you need to eat out intelligently—whether you're enjoying burgers, pizza, bagels, pasta, or burritos at your favorite restaurant. Special features include more than 2,500 menu items from more than 50 major restaurant chains, complete nutrition information for every menu item, restaurant pitfalls and strategies for defensive restaurant dining, and much more.

Nonmember: $13.95
Member: $11.95
Order #4819-01

Quick & Easy Diabetic Recipes for One
Kathleen Stanley, CDE, RD, MSED
Connie C. Crawley, MS, RD, LD

More than 100 breakfast, lunch, dinner, and snack recipes cut down to single-serving size.

Nonmember: $12.95
Member: $10.95
Order #4621-01

Month of Meals: Classic Cooking

Choose from the classic tastes of Chicken Cacciatore, Oven Fried Fish, Sloppy Joes, Shish Kabobs, Roast Leg of Lamb, Lasagna, Minestrone Soup, Grilled Cheese Sandwiches, amd many others. And just because it's Christmas doesn't mean you have to abandon your healthy meal plan. A Special Occasion section offers tips for brunches, holidays, parties, and restaurants to give you delicious dining options in any setting. 58 pages. Spiral-bound.

One Low Price: $14.95
Order #4701-01

Month of Meals: Ethnic Delights

A healthy diet doesn't have to keep you from enjoying your favorite restaurants: tips for Mexican, Italian, and Chinese restaurants are featured. Quick-to-fix and ethnic recipes are also included. Choose from Beef Burritos, Chop Suey, Veal Piccata, Stuffed Peppers, and many others. 63 pages. Spiral-bound.
One Low Price: $14.95
Order #4702-01

Month of Meals: Meals in Minutes

Eat at McDonald's, Wendy's, Taco Bell, and other fast food restaurants and still maintain a healthy diet. Special sections offer tips on planning meals when you're ill, reading ingredient labels, preparing for picnics and barbecues, more. Quick-to-fix menu choices include Seafood Stir Fry, Fajita in a Pita, Hurry-Up Beef Stew, Quick Homemade Raisin Bread, Macaroni and Cheese, many others. 80 pages. Spiral-bound.
One Low Price: $14.95
#4703-01

Month of Meals: Old-Time Favorites

Old-time family favorites like Meatloaf and Pot Roast will remind you of the irresistible meals grandma used to make. Hints for turning family-size meals into delicious "planned-overs" will keep leftovers from going to waste. Meal plans for one or two people are also featured. Choose from Oven Crispy Chicken, Beef Stroganoff, Kielbasa and Sauerkraut, Sausage and Cornbread Pie, and many others. 74 pages. Spiral-bound.
One Low Price: $14.95
Order #4704-01

Month of Meals: Vegetarian Pleasures

Choose from a garden of fresh selections like Eggplant Italian, Stuffed Zucchini, Cucumbers with Dill Dressing, Vegetable Lasagna, and many others. Craving a snack? Try Red Pepper Dip, Eggplant Caviar, or Beanito Spread. A special section shows you the most nutritious ways to cook with whole grains, and how to add flavor to your meals with peanuts, walnuts, pecans, pumpkin seeds, and more. 58 pages. Spiral-bound.
One Low Price: $14.95
Order #4705-01

Official Pocket Guide to Diabetic Exchanges

Finally! A pocket-sized version of ADA's most popular aid to balanced nutrition.
Nonmember: $5.95
Member: $4.95
Order #4709-01

The Diabetes Carbohydrate & Fat Gram Guide, 2nd Edition
Lea Ann Holzmeister, RD, CDE
Hundreds of charts list foods, serving sizes, and nutrient data for generic and packaged products.
One Low Price: $14.95
Order #4708-02

Brand-Name Diabetic Meals in Minutes
More than 200 kitchen-tested recipes from Swanson, Campbell Soup, Kraft Foods, and more.
Nonmember: $12.95
Member: $10.95
Order #4620-01

Complete Quick & Hearty Cookbook
Features dozens of simple yet delicious recipes from the best of the popular *Healthy Selects* cookbook series.
Nonmember: $12.95
Member: $10.95
Order #4624-01

Diabetic Meals in 30 Minutes or Less
Robyn Webb
Choose from more than 140 delicious, quick-to-fix meals.
Nonmember: $11.95
Member: $9.95
Order #4614-01

Diabetes Meal Planning Made Easy, 2nd Edition
Hope S. Warshaw, MMSc, RD, CDE
Discover how to master the food pyramid, understand Nutrition Facts and food labels, more.
One Low Price: $14.95
Order #4706-02

Magic Menus
Spanish Omelets, Blueberry Muffins, Oven-Fried Chicken, more.
Nonmember: $14.95
Member: $12.95
Order #4707-01

Memorable Menus
Robyn Webb
Roast Turkey Tenderloins, Honey-Mustard Chicken, Southern Shrimp Gumbo, more.
Nonmember: $19.95
Member: $17.95
Order #4619-01

Sweet Kids
Betty Page Brackenridge, MS, RD, CDE
Richard R. Rubin, PhD, CDE
Practical meal planning and nutrition advice for parents of diabetic children.
Nonmember: $11.95
Member: $9.95
Order #4905-01

Self-Care

The American Diabetes Association Complete Guide to Diabetes, 2nd Edition
American Diabetes Association
Everything you ever needed to know about diabetes contained inside one practical book—now updated! One of the most complete and authoritative resources you can find on diabetes, it covers everything from how to manage types 1 and 2 and gestational diabetes to traveling with insulin, sick day action plans, and recognizing hypoglycemia. You get in-depth coverage on preventing and treating complications, recognizing symptoms, exercising, nutrition, glucose control, sexual issues, pregnancy, and more.
Nonmember: $23.95
Member: $19.95
Order #4809-02

The Diabetes Problem Solver
Nancy Touchette, PhD
Quick: You think you may have diabetic ketoacidosis, a life-threatening condition. What are the symptoms? What should you do first? What are the treatments? How could it have been prevented? *The Diabetes Problem Solver* is the first reference guide that helps you identify and prevent the most common diabetes-related problems you encounter from day to day. From hypoglycemia, nerve pain, and foot ulcers to eye disease, depression, and eating disorders, virtually every possible problem is covered. *The Diabetes Problem Solver* addresses each problem by answering five crucial questions:

1. What are the symptoms?
2. What are the risks?
3. What do I do now?
4. What's the best treatment?
5. How can I prevent this problem?

You'll find extensive, easy-to-read coverage of just about every diabetes problem you can imagine, and comprehensive flowcharts at the front of the book lead you from symptoms to possible solutions quickly.
Nonmember: $19.95
Member: $17.95
Order #4825-01

Diabetes Burnout: What to Do When You Can't Take It Anymore
William H. Polonsky, PhD, CDE
Living with diabetes is hard work. It's easy to get discouraged, frustrated and depressed—just plain old burned out. Finally there's a book that understands the roller-coaster of emotions you go through and gives you the tools you need to keep the "downers" from overwhelming you—all in a compassionate and even humorous way. It can help you pinpoint whether you've hit diabetes burnout (if so, you're not alone!).
Nonmember: $18.95
Member: $16.95
Order #4822-01

16 Myths of a Diabetic Diet
Karen Hanson Chalmers, MS, RD, CDE
Amy E. Peterson, MS, RD, CDE
Now there's an easier way to debunk the myths you often hear, such as "you need to eat foods sweetened with sugar substitutes instead of sugar," "don't eat too many starchy foods," and "no snacking or giving in to food cravings." It's not even true that you have to eat different food from everyone else. This exciting book sets the record straight on the 16 most common myths about food and diet.
Nonmember: $14.95
Member: $12.95
Order #4829-01

101 Foot Care Tips for People with Diabetes
Jessie H. Ahroni, PhD, ARNP, CDE
"Diabetic foot problems cause more hospital stays than any other complication of diabetes. This book tells you what to do for good foot care. It can help you stand on your own two feet for a lifetime!"
—Neil M. Schaffler, DPM, FACFAS
President, Baltimore Podiatry Group

- What should I do if I nick myself while trimming my toenails?
- How can I tell whether my shoes fit?
- What should I do if I have bunions?

These are just a few of the 101 questions answered in this indispensable new book for people with diabetes.
One Low Price: $14.95
Order #4834-01

101 Medication Tips for People with Diabetes
Betsy A. Carlisle, PharmD
Mary Anne Koda-Kimble, PharmD, CDE
Lisa Kroon, PharmD

1. What is the difference between regular and lispro insulin?
2. What are the main side effects of the drugs used to treat type 2 diabetes?
3. Will my diabetes medications interact with other drugs I'm taking?
4. My doctor prescribed an "ACE inhibitor." What is this drug? What will it do?

Treating diabetes can get complicated, especially when you consider the bewildering number of medications that must be carefully integrated with diet and exercise. Here you'll find answers to 101 of the most commonly asked questions about diabetes and medication. An indispensable reference for anyone with type 1, type 2, or gestational diabetes.
One Low Price: $14.95
Order #4833-01

101 Nutrition Tips for People with Diabetes
Patti B. Geil, MS, RD, FADA, CDE
Lea Ann Holzmeister, RD, CDE

1. Which type of fiber helps my blood sugar?
2. What do I do if my toddler refuses to eat her meal?
3. If a food is sugar-free, can I eat all I want?

In this latest addition to the best-selling 101 Tips series, co-authors Patti Geil and Lea Ann Holzmeister—experts on nutrition and diabetes—use their professional experience with hundreds of patients over the years to answer the most commonly asked questions about diabetes and nutrition. You'll discover handy tips on meal planning, general nutrition, managing medication and meals, shopping and cooking, weight loss, and more.
One Low Price: $14.95
Order #4828-01

101 Tips for Improving Your Blood Sugar, 2nd Edition
David S. Schade, MD, and
The University of New Mexico Diabetes Care Team
Last night you ate a normal meal and took your usual insulin dose. When you woke up this morning you had low blood sugar. Why?

You work hard all week and you like to reward yourself by sleeping in on weekends. How can you avoid waking up with high blood sugar?

These are just a couple of the more than 100 tips you'll discover in this newly revised second edition of an ADA bestseller. Dozens of other tips—many of them just added—will help you reduce the risk of complications from extremes in blood sugar levels.
One Low Price: $14.95
Order #4805-01

101 Tips for Staying Healthy with Diabetes (& Avoiding Complications), 2nd Edition
David S. Schade, MD, and
The University of New Mexico Diabetes Care Team

1. Is testing your urine for glucose and ketones an accurate way to measure blood sugar?
2. What's the best way to reduce the pain of frequent finger sticks?
3. Will an insulin pump help you prevent complications?

These are just a few of the more than 110 tips you'll discover in this newly revised second edition of an ADA bestseller. Dozens of other tips—many of them just added—will help you reduce the risk of complications and help you lead a healthy life.
One Low Price: $14.95
Order #4810-01

Diabetes Meal Planning on $7 a Day—or Less
Patti B. Geil, MS, RD, FADA, CDE
Tami A. Ross, RD, CDE

You can save money—lots of it—without sacrificing what's most important to you: a healthy variety of great-tasting meals. Learn how to save money by planning meals more carefully, use shopping tips to save money at the grocery store, eat at your favorite restaurants economically, and much more. Each of the 100 quick and easy recipes includes cost per serving and complete nutrition information to help you create a more cost-conscious, healthy meal plan.
Nonmember: $12.95
Member: $10.95
Order #4711-01

Meditations on Diabetes
Catherine Feste

Modern medicine has come full circle to realize again what ancient healers knew: that illness affects both the body and the soul. Cathy Feste has lived with diabetes for 40 years, so she knows the physical, emotional, and spiritual challenges that come with diabetes. With every turn of the page you'll discover reassuring advice and insight in daily meditations from the author's journals with a little help from her friends, such as Ralph Waldo Emerson, Eleanor Roosevelt, Helen Keller, and many others.
Nonmember: $13.95
Member: $11.95
Order #4820-01

When Diabetes Hits Home
Wendy Satin Rapaport, LCSW, PsyD

A reassuring exploration of the full spectrum of emotional issues you and your family may struggle with throughout your lives. You'll learn how to cope with the initial period of anger and anxiety at diagnosis, develop your spiritual self and discover the meaning of living with a chronic disease, address the changes all families go through and learn how to cope with them emotionally, and much more.

Nonmember: $19.95
Member: $17.95
Order #4818-01

The Uncomplicated Guide to Diabetes Complications
Edited by Marvin E. Levin, MD
and Michael A. Pfeifer, MD

Thorough, comprehensive chapters cover everything you need to know about preventing and treating diabetes complications—in simple language that anyone can understand. All major complications and special concerns are covered, including kidney disease, heart disease, obesity, eye disease and blindness, impotence and sexual disorders, hypertension and stroke, neuropathy and vascular disease, and more.

Nonmember: $18.95
Member: $16.95
Order #4814-01

Women & Diabetes, 2nd Edition
Laurinda M. Poirier, RN, MPH, CDE
Katherine M. Coburn, MPH

Special thoughts to help a woman with diabetes move through life with confidence.

One Low Price: $14.95
Order #4907-02

Caring for the Diabetic Soul

Simple solutions for coping with the psychological challenges of diabetes.

Nonmember: $9.95
Member: $8.95
Order #4815-01

Winning with Diabetes

Inspiring true stories of people who live life to the fullest, despite having diabetes.

Nonmember: $12.95
Member: $10.95
Order #4824-01

Dear Diabetes Advisor
Michael A. Pfeifer, MD, CDE

Solid, no-nonsense answers to commonsense questions about diabetes.

Nonmember: $9.95
Member: $8.95
Order #4813-01

Type 2 Diabetes: Your Healthy Living Guide, 2nd Edition
A thorough guide to staying healthy with type 2 diabetes.
Nonmember: $16.95
Member: $14.95
Order #4804-01

The Commonsense Guide to Weight Loss
Barbara Caleen Hansen, PhD
Shauna S. Roberts, PhD
Learn how to lose weight—and keep it off—using medically proven techniques from the weight-loss experts. You'll discover the seven crucial elements of weight loss for people with diabetes, including how to choose the right target weight; make permanent lifestyle changes; measure weight-loss progress by tracking health, not weight; develop a healthy meal plan; maintain an active lifestyle and more.
One Low Price: $19.95
Order #4816-01

The Complete Weight Loss Workbook
Judith Wylie-Rosett, EdD, RD
Charles Swencionis, PhD
Arlene Caban, BS
Allison J. Friedler, BS
Nicole Schaffer, MA
Proven techniques for controlling weight-related health problems. The authors devised a unique workbook that offers a series of checklists, worksheets, mini-cases, calculation exercises, mental reminders, and other practical aids to knocking off those extra pounds and staying fit for good.
Features real-life examples of people who illustrate and explain the patterns that lead to success or failure in watching your weight.
Nonmember: $19.95
Member: $17.95
Order #4812-01

Diabetes & Pregnancy: What to Expect
Learn about an unborn baby's development, tests to expect, labor and delivery, and more.
Nonmember: $9.95
Member: $8.95
Order #4903-01

Order Toll-Free: 1-800-232-6733

About the American Diabetes Association

The American Diabetes Association is the nation's leading voluntary health organization supporting diabetes research, information, and advocacy. Its mission is to prevent and cure diabetes and to improve the lives of all people affected by diabetes. The American Diabetes Association is the leading publisher of comprehensive diabetes information. Its huge library of practical and authoritative books for people with diabetes covers every aspect of self-care—cooking and nutrition, fitness, weight control, medications, complications, emotional issues, and general self-care.

To order American Diabetes Association books: Call 1-800-232-6733. http://store.diabetes.org (Note: there is no need to use **www** when typing this particular Web address.)

To join the American Diabetes Association: Call 1-800-806-7801. www.diabetes.org/membership

For more information about diabetes or ADA programs and services: Call 1-800-342-2383. E-mail: Customerservice@diabetes.org www.diabetes.org

To locate an ADA/NCQA Recognized Provider of quality diabetes care in your area: www.ncqa.org/dprp

To find an ADA Recognized Education Program in your area: Call 1-888-232-0822. www.diabetes.org/recognition/education.asp

To join the fight to increase funding for diabetes research, end discrimination, and improve insurance coverage: Call 1-800-342-2383. www.diabetes.org/advocacy

To find out how you can get involved with the programs in your community: Call 1-800-342-2383. See below for program Web addresses.

- *American Diabetes Month:* Educational activities aimed at those diagnosed with diabetes—month of November. www.diabetes.org/ADM

- *American Diabetes Alert:* Annual public awareness campaign to find the undiagnosed—held the fourth Tuesday in March. www.diabetes.org/alert

- *The Diabetes Assistance & Resources Program (DAR):* diabetes awareness program targeted to the Latino community. www.diabetes.org/DAR

- *African American Program:* diabetes awareness program targeted to the African American community. www.diabetes.org/africanamerican

- *Awakening the Spirit: Pathways to Diabetes Prevention & Control:* diabetes awareness program targeted to the Native American community. www.diabetes.org/awakening

To find out about an important research project regarding type 2 diabetes: www.diabetes.org/ada/research.asp

To obtain information on making a planned gift or charitable bequest: Call 1-888-700-7029. www.diabetes.org/ada/plan.asp

To make a donation or memorial contribution: Call 1-800-342-2383. www.diabetes.org/ada/cont.asp